C000130429

Steam Around the Fells

MICHAEL WELCH

Rails

ISBN 978 1 85414 457 7

Published by
Rails Publishing
www.capitaltransport.com

Printed in the India

© Michael Welch 2021

Front cover: The last few yards to Ais Gill. Stanier Class 5MT No.44983 makes light work of the last stretch of the climb with the 12.40pm Carlisle to Stourton express freight, blotting out Wild Boar Fell in the process. This portrait was taken in August 1964. *Peter Robinson*

Title page: Following reconstruction of the roof in the 1950s, Carlisle Citadel station was light and airy as exemplified here in this picture which dates from 1964. The train depicted is a special, titled 'The Great Cumberland Railroad Rave', which was conveying jazz enthusiasts to Keswick, the formation including parcels vans fitted out as dance halls or bars. Nicely cleaned Ivatt Class 2MT 2-6-0s Nos. 46458 and 46434 are in charge. Seven main line routes converged on the Border City at that time, plus the branch to Silloth, and it enjoyed unrivalled status as Cumberland's premier railway centre. *Peter Robinson*

Back cover: Stanier 'Royal Scot' Class 7P 4-6-0 No.46133 *The Green Howards* heads a Manchester to Glasgow express through the Lune gorge on 18th August 1962. Based at Leeds (Holbeck) shed for most of the 1950s, No.46133 was moved to Kentish Town in 1958 and returned north to Newton Heath in 1961 from where it was withdrawn in February 1963. *Gavin Morrison*

Introduction

In the late 1950s I lived on the South Coast where most train services were provided by electric units, so it was not exciting territory for an enthusiastic train spotter. The highlight of my year were the summer school breaks, spent at my grandmother's home in Droylsden just outside Manchester, my base for the duration of the holidays. The 'Royal Scots', 'Jubilees' and 'Black Fives' on offer, and the demanding routes over which they worked, always seemed more impressive to me than the steam traction south of the river Thames. During the summer of 1960 my notebook records visits to York, Doncaster, Derby and Crewe while on Sundays a tour of local engine sheds was imperative: after all, there would be hundreds of locomotives on view, including visitors from afar.

The Divisional Passenger Manager in Manchester published a pamphlet outlining special fares available to racegoers using scheduled services and, by a remarkable stroke of luck, many courses were in ideal locations for an avid spotter. In 1961 I became more adventurous and my first recorded visit to Carlisle was made on 29th July, motive power being Polmadie-based 'Royal Scot' No.46104 *Scottish Borderer* on the 9.30am from Victoria. Manchester is located in a dip and there is an arduous climb to Bolton, and No.46104 was piloted to that point by Stanier 2-6-4T No.42633. My notes also record that Fairburn 2-6-4T No.42238 assisted *Scottish Borderer* from Oxenholme for the climbs up to Grayrigg and Shap summit, where it was presumably detached. Could I have wished for a more fascinating journey? During the journey my notebook was in constant use recording the engine numbers and, predictably perhaps, the most common were those of the very numerous Stanier Class 5MT locomotives. The most interesting sighting at Preston was that of No.47008, a short-wheelbase 0-4-0ST built at Horwich Works in 1953; it was similar to Stanier's design for the LMS originally introduced in 1932 for dock shunting. One of the first locomotives noted on arrival at Carlisle was Gresley Class A3 No.60093 *Coronach* which I suspect had just arrived on the 'Waverley' from Edinburgh. This was one of four allocated to Carlisle (Canal) shed at that time for duties on the legendary Waverley route to the Scottish capital. Normally confined to that route, apart from scheduled visits to main works for overhaul, those locomotives rarely visited other locations south of the border, and I was to see other representatives later, during my visit to Canal shed.

An absolutely indispensable publication at that time as far as railway enthusiasts were concerned was 'The British Locomotive Shed Directory' which was, to quote the blurb on the front cover, 'a complete guide to all main line locomotive sheds and works in Great Britain'. The guide was apparently published privately by a gentleman living in Birmingham and many thousands of spotters doubtless treasured their copy which gave precise details of how to reach sheds, and even included invaluable maps of city centres for the uninitiated. Naturally, I wanted to see as many locomotives as possible during my first visit to the Border City and, aided by the invaluable Shed Directory, I set off for Upperby shed which was a straightforward 20-minute walk along London Road. My walk was rewarded by the sight of 28 steam locomotives, including two 'Princess Coronation' Pacifics, a 'Royal Scot' and five 'Jubilees'.

No doubt buoyed by my success at Upperby, I now decided to try my luck at the much larger Kingmoor shed, located 1½ miles north of Citadel station, but the 45-minute walk sounded a bit daunting. The Shed Directory once again proved its worth, advising that a C3 or C4 St. Anns bus ran from English Street to the end of Etterby Road, from where a broad cinder path led to the shed. The big question was, however, would I be able to get into the shed which I knew would be very busy with locomotives moving about and, no doubt, piles of hot ash providing a considerable danger to the unwary? In the event I strolled down the cinder path unchallenged and it was likely the shed staff had long since given up trying to eject unauthorised visitors such as myself, and intimidating 'Trespassers Will Be Prosecuted' notices could be safely ignored. The Shed Directory had not mentioned that a constant pall of black smoke hung over the shed, the location of which could probably be seen for miles around. However, my elation on reaching the shed yard was soon tempered by the sad sight of two forlorn 'Princess Royal' Pacifics with sacks over their chimneys on the stored row of engines that also included an extremely rusty Caledonian Railway locomotive, No.57653. One of the Pacifics, No.46201 *Princess Elizabeth* was returned to traffic in early 1962 as a result of a motive power shortage and was subsequently preserved, but No.46210 *Lady Patricia* was withdrawn a few months after my visit and cut-up in May 1962. A 'Princess Coronation' class locomotive from Glasgow (Polmadie) shed, No.46223 *Princess Alice*, was noted plus a dozen 'Jubilees', nearly all of which were based at Kingmoor, and the remainder of the locomotives consisted largely of 'Black Fives', Hughes/Fowler 'Crabs' and miscellaneous local shunting engines. All in all, I had jotted down no fewer than 89 numbers, not bad for a Saturday at the height of the summer, and probably a total of well over 100 would have been 'on shed' the following day.

I knew that the next shed on my list, the former North British Railway Carlisle (Canal) depot, was much smaller than the other two but in many respects could be the most interesting, with a selection of former LNER types on the allocation including Class A3 Pacifics. Perhaps it was my lucky day because two A3s, Nos.60079 *Bayardo*, which is illustrated elsewhere in this album, and 60097 *Humorist* were on shed accompanied by Class V2 2-6-2s, B1 4-6-0s and even one or two ancient J36 0-6-0s that were presumably used on local yard shunting and suchlike. All too soon my Carlisle adventure was over and I guess I would have returned 'home' on the 4.30pm from Glasgow which departed from Carlisle at 6.54pm and arrived at Manchester (Victoria) at 9.37pm. I think that was the trip when I was rashly leaning out of a window as the train hurtled down from Shap summit and paid the price when I got a soaking when it hit the troughs at Dillcar. Happy days indeed.

During the compilation of this album Bob Dalton, Chris Evans, Dave Fakes and Terry Phillips have offered much constructive criticism and suggested many worthwhile amendments and improvements to the text and thanks are due to those gentlemen. In addition, Richard Barber (Armstrong Railway Photographic Trust), John Chalcraft (Rail Photoprints), Peter Robinson (Bob Leslie collection) and Phil Tuer (Cumbrian Railways Association) have kindly made available photographs from the collections in their care, for which I am most grateful.

Michael Welch
Burgess Hill
West Sussex
January 2021

Contents

The eminent railway builder Joseph Locke is said to have once stood on the battlements of Lancaster castle shielding his eyes as he gazed at the continuous range of mountains that stretched from the Cumberland coast to the Pennine Chain. The precise date of that occurrence has not been recorded but what is generally accepted is the fact that Locke, together with George Stephenson, visited the area in 1836, the former surveying on behalf of the Grand Junction Railway which had a route to Scotland as its major objective. The latter was seeking a route for the Maryport & Carlisle Railway and their different aims, coupled with their already strained relationship following disagreements during the building of the Liverpool & Manchester Railway, later led to a permanent breach. Rather than cross the forbidding mountains, Stephenson's plan was to avoid them entirely by constructing a barrage across Morecambe Bay and from there across the Duddon estuary. From there the line would continue to Bootle, St. Bees and eventually link up with a projected extension of the Maryport & Carlisle Railway. Stephenson extolled the virtues of this idea by pointing out that the route was free from heavy gradients and connected with many towns and harbours whereas a line through the Lune gorge and over Shap summit would be prone to blockage during the wintertime.

Locke was scornful of these assertions and pressed on with his bold ideas but came under intense pressure from various local interests and proposed two routes between Tebay and Penrith in order to avoid tunnelling. The citizens of Kendal meanwhile, led by Cornelius Nelson, a well known public benefactor and local mill owner, were vociferous in their demand that the line should serve their town and proposed a route across the river Kent and through Longsleddale, a ravine-like valley surrounded by rugged peaks. From there this spectacular route would have plunged under Gatescarth Pass in a two miles-long tunnel, emerging on the shores of Haweswater from where it would have descended to join Locke's route at Bampton. In stark contrast the inhabitants of the Vale of Lune were vehemently opposed to any idea of a railway which would 'materially injure many private grounds', and they passed three critical resolutions during a meeting at the Royal Hotel, Kirkby Lonsdale. In March 1842 Locke decided to submit two alternative routes to Parliament, one via Oxenholme and Tebay to Penrith and another through the Vale of Lune via Kirkby Lonsdale, while the obvious disadvantages of the line through Longsleddale

effectively ruled it out of the running. Plans were already being formulated for a line to Scotland over Beattock summit at this time and there was the challenge of the East Coast route in the background. There were many obstacles to be sorted out including finance, but in late 1842 it was announced that 'southern companies', no doubt including the Grand Junction Railway, would provide £500,000 if a similar amount could be raised locally in Cumberland. The powerful Lord Lonsdale was initially opposed to the line due to its close proximity to his castle but even he relented. The great day eventually came when, on 5th June 1844, the Bill for the construction of the line passed through Parliament unopposed and, remarkably, the first sod was cut near Birkbeck viaduct only a month later. The man in charge of the works was the legendary civil engineer Thomas Brassey who had already gained much experience as a pioneer of railway building. Due to its geographical location Kendal was bypassed but at least Locke opted to serve the town by taking the rails through nearby Oxenholme, and his other crucial decision was to lay the tracks across Shap Fell in order to reduce construction costs. In the photo on the previous page, Oxenholme station is depicted with BR Standard 'Britannia' Pacific No.70011 *Hotspur* passing through at the head of a southbound goods working on 7th March 1964. The station was built in a relatively remote location and only two houses, on the hill on the right, are visible. *Gordon Edgar / Rail Photoprints collection*

Above: The photographer's lucky day. Apart from a very short downhill stretch near Burton & Holme, trains heading north on the West Coast Main Line climb all of the way from Carnforth, virtually at sea level, to Shap summit high up in the fells. In this shot Stanier 'Jubilee' Class 6P/5F 4-6-0 No.45595 *Southern Rhodesia* is already hard at work battling the 1 in 178 gradient through Oxenholme station at the head of a Birmingham to Edinburgh train on 8th September 1961. The rather gloomy, gas-lit station premises are apparent in this view, the Windermere branch platform being visible on the right. Four locomotives of this class originally carried plaques with the nameplate but by the date of this picture *Southern Rhodesia* was the only engine to retain it, so it really was a lucky shot. *Noel Machell*

Lambrigg crossing signal box, just visible in the background, was a small intermediate block post, one of four between Oxenholme and the top of the first summit at Grayrigg which divided the line into short sections, thereby assisting the flow of traffic. Lambrigg survived to become the last intermediate box on this section, doubtless due to its dual role controlling a level crossing on a minor country lane. Most photographs taken on this section would normally feature heavy passenger or goods trains charging uphill but here is a picture of a local civil engineer's train headed by a filthy Ivatt Class 4MT 2-6-0 No.43073. The gradient is 1 in 106 at this point and the locomotive certainly seems to have a struggle on its hands. This photograph was taken on a typically misty Lake District day in 1966.
Alan Orchard / Gordon Edgar collection

The driver of Stanier Class 5MT No.45395, working a heavy freight train, clearly had confidence in his steed and decided to tackle the bank up to Grayrigg without assistance, quite a risky proposition. The Class 5MT was photographed going great guns at Hardrigg on 3rd June 1966. No.45395 was obviously just *ex*-works and there is hardly a trace of leaking steam at the front end and they may have been factors in the driver's decision. During this period most steam locomotives were in deplorable external condition and the sight of this immaculate 'Black Five' must have really brightened up the photographer's day. *Hugh Ballantyne / Rail Photoprints collection*

Grayrigg bank is famous among the railway enthusiast fraternity but, perhaps, not so well known is the fact that there used to be a station at the summit which served a small hamlet situated just over a mile away on the A6 trunk road. Any local travellers would probably have taken the bus to Kendal rather than traipse down the moorland road to the station and this, no doubt, was a factor in the decision to close Grayrigg station which occurred from 1st February 1954. BR was in no hurry to demolish the premises, however, and the London-bound platform plus a building on the northbound platform were still in evidence when this shot of 'Black Five' No.45434 was taken on 12th June 1964. *Rodney Lissenden*

Two heads are better than one. Northbound trains sometimes took a pilot locomotive from Oxenholme, where there was a small sub depot, to Shap summit where it would be detached. In this photograph Stanier Class 4MT No.42449 is seen assisting rebuilt 'Patriot' 4-6-0 No.45512 *Bunsen* between the former Grayrigg station and Low Gill on 12th July 1964. There is a short downhill section at this point but, even so, the locomotives appear to be working very hard, perhaps with a view to gaining momentum prior to their assault on Shap bank. One can only imagine the tremendous sound being emitted by the two locomotives as they passed the photographer's viewpoint. Memories, as they say, are made of this. *Steve Armitage / Rail Photoprints collection*

Stanier 'Royal Scot' Class 7P 4-6-0 No.46106 *Gordon Highlander* was a unique locomotive because it was fitted with straight-sided smoke deflectors. Here it is depicted approaching Low Gill with a lightweight summer Saturday extra from Blackpool to Glasgow on 18th August 1962. The line from Clapham Junction and Ingleton converged with the West Coast Main Line at Low Gill but lost its passenger service from 1st February 1954, though it remained open for goods traffic and the occasional diverted passenger train until the early 1960s. Low Gill station, however, which was in a remote location far from any centres of population, managed to retain its meagre passenger service until 7th March 1960. *Gavin Morrison*

Photographs of Stanier 'Princess Royal' Class 8P Pacifics working over the Shap route are hard to find mainly due to the fact that some of the engines of this small class were based at Edge Hill shed for Liverpool expresses, whilst others were often employed on Anglo-Scottish night time sleeping car trains. Here, in this scene photographed in 1955, No.46209 *Princess Beatrice* is seen threading the Lune gorge in charge of 'The Mid-Day Scot', the meandering river being visible on the left of the picture. In the 1959 timetable this train was advertised to leave London at 1.20pm on Mondays to Fridays, the scheduled arrival time in Glasgow being 9.10pm with stops at Rugby, Crewe, Carlisle and Carstairs. On Saturdays the journey time was extended by 35 minutes, presumably due to engineering works. *Rail Photoprints collection*

Wet days in the Lake District are not unheard of, and it has been known for railway photographers who stood too close to Dillicar troughs when a locomotive was picking up water at speed to get thoroughly soaked even when it wasn't raining. It looks as though 11th August 1962 was a particularly nasty day in the area and the fells are hidden from view as Fowler Class 4MT 2-6-4T No.42319, piloting an unidentified 'Jubilee' Class 4-6-0, has just passed over the troughs which are visible in the background. No.42319 was based at Carnforth at the time of the photograph and would have no doubt been attached at Oxenholme to provide assistance as far as Shap summit.
Rail Photoprints

The last days of steam at Tebay shed. The London & North Western Railway constructed a shed at Tebay in 1861 to cater for increased traffic following the inauguration of services across the Pennines to Barnard Castle. Built of stone, the shed had a timber frame roof and in the 1920s there was an allocation of around 20 locomotives. By the mid-1930s the premises were in a dilapidated condition and little of the original roof was still *in situ,* so working there in such primitive conditions during the winter must have been extremely unpleasant. The shed was rebuilt in the late 1940s, not before time some folk might say, and a much needed roof was doubtless top of the list of the improvements. In the mid-1950s BR installed a new coal and ash plant together with a 60ft. diameter turntable. By this time, however, the shed's duties had dwindled, a process that continued when the Stainmore route over the Pennines was closed to passenger services in early 1962. Steam banking up to Shap summit ceased in December 1967 following the elimination of steam traction in Carlisle but by that date only a token allocation of five BR Standard Class 4MT 4-6-0s remained. Two of those machines, Nos.75037 and 75039, can be seen in this panoramic study of Tebay shed which was taken on 10th July 1967. Four gentlemen can be seen on the left, no doubt amazed by the antics of the photographer apparently perched on top of the depot's coaling plant. Note the bank of long civil engineer's sidings in the background which are largely hidden from view and rarely feature in photographs. *John Goss*

A picture showing part of the massive, stone-built train shed at Tebay which covered the easternmost platform. The village of Tebay was almost a mile away to the north but a small railway community existed around the station, this consisting of a number of terraces of the type seen here. The shiny *ex*-works locomotive is Ivatt Class 2MT No.46471, of Kirkby Stephen shed, which was new at the time, having been out-shopped from Darlington works in July 1951. *Rail Photoprints collection*

A fascinating view of the south end of Tebay station in 1952 with unrebuilt Stanier 'Royal Scot' Class 7P 4-6-0 No.6151 *The Royal Horse Guardsman* pausing with a southbound train. Following the successful rebuilding of two of his 'Jubilee' Class 4-6-0s with taper boilers, double chimneys and new cylinders in 1942 Stanier introduced a rebuilt version of the 'Royal Scots' with the same improvements and the entire class was similarly treated between 1943 and 1955. This vintage photograph illustrates the massive tunnel-like train shed which towered over the Kirkby Stephen line platform which, presumably, could sometimes become filled with smoke. It must have been a very gloomy and forbidding place to wait for a train, but 1952 was the last year of regular passenger trains over the line though seasonal workings continued until September 1961. The top of Tebay's up starting signal (not in the picture!) was a godsend to drivers of trains coming down the bank from Shap and must have been visible for some considerable distance. *Rail Photoprints collection*

A general view of the north end of Tebay station with Stanier Class 5MT No.44911 taking a ballast train through the station on 17th June 1967. The station buildings on the northbound platform were also very substantially constructed, like those on the opposite side of the premises, and had a castellated appearance. There used to be canopies on both platforms but they were removed sometime during the 1950s. Part of Tebay shed's coaling plant can just be seen while the front end of a BR Standard Class 4MT on banking duty is also visible. *John Goss*

Timekeeping has always been of the utmost importance on the West Coast main line and it was therefore essential that Tebay station's clock was always showing the correct time. Here, a member of staff balances precariously on a strategically positioned platform bench to set the station's clock on 15th July 1967. Today, in these health and safety conscious times an approved step ladder would be mandatory, the person would have to be fully certified to undertake the task and wear a full length high visibility vest while carrying out the job. In addition, of course, another member of staff would have to be present just in case something went wrong. Perhaps a safety harness, goggles and a hard hat would also be required. In such circumstances the local manager would probably come to the conclusion that 'maintaining' the timepiece was so expensive it would have to be removed. *John Goss*

Steam's West Coast swan song. During the summer of 1967 steam traction was prominent on summer Saturday 'dated' trains over Shap summit and six northbound and five southbound workings were regularly steam hauled by either Stanier 'Black Fives' or 'Britannia' Pacifics. Many trains changed locomotives at Carlisle where the platforms were sometimes thronged with enthusiasts anxious to obtain photographs or have a run behind steam traction whilst there was still the opportunity. A particularly interesting working was the 6.40am SO Birmingham to Glasgow, which travelled over the Settle & Carlisle line, and was regularly steam hauled north of the border despite the Scottish Region making it clear that steam locomotives were no longer welcome in its territory. In addition to the advertised busy Saturday service many relief trains were also provided and it is recorded that on 29th July, which marked the end of the Glasgow holidays, a total of 14 relief trains ran thus placing an enormous strain on motive power resources. The Birmingham train was not the only one to be steam-hauled into Scotland on that day because the 1.27pm Manchester Victoria to Glasgow Central continued northwards from Carlisle behind 'Britannia' No.70038 *Robin Hood*, indicating a desperate shortage of engines. One of the Saturday 'dated' workings booked for steam was the 8.25am Morecambe to Glasgow which is seen here passing Tebay behind Class 5MT No.45209 before assaulting the climb to Shap summit. *Author*

High summer at Tebay. Class WD 2-8-0 No.90119, assisted in the rear by a 2-6-4T, begins the slow grind up to Shap summit on 29th June 1964. A total of 935 of these war-time 'Austerity' locomotives was built by the North British Locomotive Company (NB) and Vulcan Foundry (VF) from 1943 onwards and many saw service in mainland Europe as part of the Allied war effort. The London & North Eastern Railway purchased 200 examples in 1947 while another 533 were on loan to BR at the time of nationalisation and purchased at the end of 1948. The NB machines were numbered 90000 to 90421 while the VF locomotives became 90422 to 90732. These were the unsung, unglamorous workhorses of heavy freight haulage and were overlooked when voluntary railway preservation took off in the mid-1960s, with the result that none of the BR locomotives was saved. This omission was rectified in 1973, however, when WD No.79257, which had become Swedish Railways No.1931, was repatriated for use on the Keighley & Worth Valley Railway in West Yorkshire. *Rodney Lissenden*

Deep winter at Tebay. The fells present a splendid spectacle carpeted in snow and in this portrait the magnificent backdrop is considerably enhanced by the sight of an unidentified Stanier 'Black Five' starting the ascent with a 2-6-4T banking at the rear: this shot was taken in 1953. The long rakes of wagons in the background mark the course of the line to Kirkby Stephen while a small part of the erstwhile 'North Eastern' engine shed is also discernible. The houses cluster around the station and, no doubt, at the time of this picture virtually everyone would have worked on the railway. *Rail Photoprints collection*

The crew of Stanier 'Princess Coronation' Pacific No.46242 *City of Glasgow* had obviously declined the services of a banking locomotive and No.46242 appears to be taking the 1 in 75 incline past Greenholme in its stride in this shot thought to date from 1962. The rear coaches of the train are still on Birkbeck viaduct which is hidden from view. *Rail Photoprints collection*

Almost effortless. Stanier 'Princess Royal' Pacific No.46209 *Princess Beatrice* was still 'blowing off' at the halfway point on the climb to Shap summit as it approached Scout Green signal box with a heavy 12-coach train some time in the 1950s. In the early 1960s the West Coast main line was flooded with English Electric Type 4 diesel locomotives and No.46209, together with all of its sister engines, was placed in store in early 1961 as 'surplus to requirements'. Most of the locomotives were returned to service for the summer and it is recorded that *Princess Beatrice* powered the 4.05pm Euston to Holyhead on 25th June. No.46209 was returned to store at the end of the summer timetable and in the autumn six members of the class were withdrawn from traffic. No. 46209 was more fortunate, however, and was once again returned to service, this time as a result of a motive power shortage in early 1962. This charmed life could not last forever and it was eventually withdrawn in September and broken up two months later. Fortunately, two representatives of this impressive class have survived into preservation. *Rail Photoprints*

The sheep in the field on the left carried on grazing, apparently unconcerned by the passage of a northbound train blasting up the bank towards Shap summit just a few yards away. Obviously, an experienced animal that had become accustomed to the deafening exhaust noise of steam locomotives heaving heavy trains up the incline. The train engine is unrebuilt 'Patriot' Class 6P5F No.45507 *Royal Tank Corps* and the machine at the back pushing for all it was worth is Fowler Class 4P 2-6-4T No.42403. The locomotive seen in the previous picture was one of the most powerful express passenger engines ever built in Great Britain and No.45507 was not in the same league, hence it required the vigorous help of a banking engine from Tebay. The tiny Scout Green signal box is just visible above the roof of the permanent way hut. The coaches forming the train are a motley selection, mostly of Gresley design, but the carriage immediately behind the locomotive is a BR Standard first class vehicle; it is in excellent condition and possibly brand new. This picture was taken on 27th July 1957. *Bob Leslie/ Peter Robinson collection*

Puffy clouds scud across the sky in this classic scene from the early 1950s recorded near Shap Wells. A northbound express headed by 'Princess Coronation' Pacific No.46226 *Duchess of Norfolk* heads towards the summit with a heavy train made up largely of LMSR stock, apart from the Great Western-designed vehicle immediately behind the locomotive: the latter was probably a through coach from Plymouth to Glasgow. No.46226 appears to be in fine fettle: note there is no trace of leaking steam at the front end despite the fact that it was being worked to the limit up the 1 in 75 gradient. The sloping smokebox indicates that *Duchess of Norfolk* was fitted with streamlined casing. *Cumbrian Railways Association*

The section of line between Tebay and Shap summit attracted hordes of photographers despite its relatively remote location in the wilds of Westmorland. The Shap Wells hotel was near to the more popular photographic spots and it is said that some of the more affluent enthusiasts stayed there during their photographic safaris. Perhaps there was a bar open to the public where other photographers could take refuge when weather conditions on the fells became particularly violent. There was no such problem on 16th June 1962 when the fells were bathed in glorious sunshine as WD Class 2-8-0 No.90157, assisted at the rear by Fowler 2-6-4T No.42414, plods up the hill to Shap summit. The photographer comments that WD Class engines were uncommon on the Shap route, Stanier Class 8Fs and 5MTs being the staple motive power on heavy freights. No.90157, however, was based at Tebay for 15 months from March 1961 specifically for the transport of stone from local quarries to Carlisle for the construction of the new marshalling yard at Kingmoor. This must have been one of its last duties working from Tebay because it was transferred to Birkenhead shed later the same month. *Noel Machell*

Maximum effort. Rebuilt 'Patriot' Class 7P No.45545 *Planet* raises the echoes as it assaults the climb towards Shap summit on 25th July 1963. Originally constructed in March 1934 at Crewe works, No.45545 was one of 18 examples of this class rebuilt by Ivatt between 1946 and 1949. They were fitted with larger taper boilers, new cylinders and double chimneys and were very similar to the rebuilt 'Royal Scots' in appearance; enginemen generally considered the rebuilt 'Patriots' to be as powerful and often better riding engines. *Planet* was taken out of service in June 1964 and broken-up for scrap five months later. *Rodney Lissenden*

Opposite: Almost there. The incredible sight and sound of steam locomotives heaving heavy trains up the steep bank from Tebay proved an irresistible draw for generations of enthusiasts and in this illustration Stanier 'Jubilee' No.45663 *Jervis* is emitting a magnificent pall of black smoke as it attacks the last few yards to the summit on 27th July 1963. What more could a railway photographer ask for? Note that there is no trace of leaking steam at the locomotive's front end and it is even 'blowing off' after such a demanding ascent. *Rodney Lissenden*

Above: Ten BR Standard Class 9F locomotives, Nos. 92020 to 92029, were built in 1955 with Franco Crosti boilers which were intended to reduce coal consumption. These boilers were an unusual arrangement whereby the smokebox chimney was used only for lighting up purposes, the normal exhaust being emitted from a separate outlet on the side of the boiler. The anticipated economies in coal consumption were disappointing, however, and the boilers suffered severe corrosion so the decision was taken to convert the locomotives to orthodox operation. The locomotives spent periods in store before being modified to conventional operation between 1959 and 1962 and were subsequently re-classified 8F because the boiler was smaller than that on the standard members of the class. Here No.92021 is depicted leaving the up loop at Shap summit in 1964; note the dainty lower quadrant signal. *ARPT*

A shift at Shap Summit signal box on a busy summer Saturday must have been a very stressful, and at times quite hectic, experience for the signalman who was responsible for ensuring that banking engines were quickly returned to Tebay in addition, of course, to controlling the movement of passenger traffic on the main line. His duties would also have included recording each movement in the train register so it would seem a break for lunch was out of the question, but perhaps he had an assistant to make life more tolerable. Here, Stanier 'Princess Coronation' Class 8P No.46251 *City of Nottingham* drifts past the box with an up express on 20th July 1963. Photographs of trains charging up the bank are plentiful but few pictures that include Shap Summit box were submitted for inclusion in this album, so the author was especially pleased when this shot was offered. *Rodney Lissenden*

Many steam aficionados considered the 'Clan' Pacifics to be the most handsome of the BR Standard designs but the enginemen who drove and fired them are likely to have taken a different view. The locomotives were a lighter version of the 'Britannias', with smaller diameter boilers and higher running plates, but they were often disappointing performers and compared unfavourably with their slightly larger sisters. A total of ten machines was built, divided between the London Midland (LMR) and Scottish regions (ScR) and it was planned to build a further fifteen, including five for the Southern Region, with the remainder destined for Scotland, but the order was cancelled. The locomotives were all built at Crewe and were out-shopped between December 1951 and April 1952. The five machines based on the ScR had a brief working career, all being withdrawn at the end of 1962 in the holocaust of steam motive power that preceded the formation of the British Railways Board, but the LMR-allocated locomotives were taken out of service one by one, presumably as overhauls became due. The last survivor was No.72006 *Clan Mackenzie* which survived until May 1966, but it was often to be found on secondary passenger duties such as hauling lightweight Carlisle to Bradford (Forster Square) stopping trains. The locomotive depicted here, No.72004 *Clan Macdonald*, of Glasgow (Polmadie) shed, was certainly earning its keep when photographed passing Shap station some time in 1960 with an eleven-coach load. The ScR based locomotives frequently powered Glasgow to Manchester (Victoria) trains and this working was probably one of those. *The late Derek Cross / Rail Photoprints collection*

Stanier Class 5MT No.44825 takes a southbound van train through Shap station on a sunny 22nd July 1967. Closure proposals for the local stations between Carnforth and Carlisle had already been published by this date and the year 1967 proved to be their last full year of operation, passenger services being withdrawn from 1st July 1968. The train service on offer from Shap at this time could not be described as generous or attractive and consisted of three up trains to Carnforth and two down trains to Carlisle; one of the former was a through service to London but there was no advertised return train. The station was lit solely by oil lamps and alighting there in the pitch black on a winter's night with flickering oil lamps being the only illumination must have been quite an experience. At least there was a footbridge so passengers did not have to cross the line in the dark, and also the luxury of a canopy on the down platform so they could shelter from the wind and rain. *Gordon Edgar / Rail Photoprints collection*

A distinctive machine. An evocative action shot of 'Princess Royal' Pacific No.46205 *Princess Victoria* pounding past Harrison's sidings on the climb to Shap with the morning Glasgow to Birmingham train on 19th May 1959. A modified valve motion was fitted to this locomotive in 1937 when its two sets of inside Walschaerts valve gear were removed and replaced with rocking shafts which enabled the outside valve motion to work the valves of the inside cylinders. The original valve motion arrangement was restored in 1955 but the heavy outside motion brackets remained *in situ* until the locomotive was withdrawn from traffic in the first cull of these fine locomotives which occurred in November 1961. *Gavin Morrison*

Southbound trains on the WCML face an 8½ miles-long climb at 1 in 125/142 from just before Eden Valley junction (where the line to Appleby diverged) to the site of Shap station, where there is short level stretch, before the climb resumes once again until the summit was reached. Thrimby Grange is about halfway up the incline and here unrebuilt 'Patriot' No.45541 *Duke of Sutherland* and 'Jubilee' No.45706 *Express*, powering a massive 15-coach Glasgow to Liverpool/Manchester train, are at grips with the ascent on 8th August 1954. Note the very tidy condition of the permanent way, particularly the neat edge to the ballast indicating the pride the staff took in the appearance of their 'length' of track. *Bob Leslie/Peter Robinson collection*

On 15th February 1964 Carlisle United were due to play Preston North End in an effort to reach the quarter finals of the FA Cup and the staff at Upperby shed rose to the occasion by turning out 'Princess Coronation' Pacific No.46238 *City of Carlisle* in absolutely sparkling condition to work the special train, run for fans. Here, the beautifully prepared locomotive is seen crossing Clifton viaduct, about three miles south of Penrith, on a glorious winter's morning with 14 coaches in tow. Withdrawn from traffic in September 1964, this magnificent machine was one of eight members of the class sold to the Troon Shipbreaking Company, Ayrshire, and cut up with almost indecent haste in December 1964. Alas, Carlisle's supporters returned home in a gloomy mood following a 1-0 defeat. *Peter Robinson*

A frustrating day. On 15th July 1967 a pair of Ivatt Class 4MT 2-6-0s worked the annual Keswick convention special from London down the remaining stub of the Penrith to Workington line as far as Keswick, and provided a very rare opportunity for enthusiasts to photograph a steam working on this wonderfully scenic route. Railway photographers hoped for a repeat performance the following Saturday when the convention participants returned to the capital and some effort was made to clean Ivatt 2-6-0 No.43139 which had been rostered for the job. Unfortunately, English Electric Type 4 No.D313 was booked to double-head with the Ivatt locomotive and the enthusiasts no doubt hoped that at least the steam locomotive would pilot the diesel on the way back from Keswick. Alas, it was not to be, and No.D313 was the leading locomotive when the train returned to Penrith, so the cleaning efforts were totally wasted. Here, No.43139, running tender first, is depicted leaving Penrith with the empty stock of the special with the diesel marshalled as train engine. *Chris Davies / Rail Photoprints collection*

Hauling an enormous van train, which were a feature of operations on the WCML, unrebuilt 'Patriot' Class 6P5F 4-6-0 No.45513 is depicted at the junction where the line from Workington and Keswick converged with the main line south of Penrith station. The first three vehicles in the formation are BR Standard General Utility Vans, commonly known in railwaymen's parlance as 'GUVs'. This photograph was taken on 31st July 1958. *Bob Leslie / Peter Robinson collection*

Opposite top: In days gone by Penrith (for Ullswater) was a moderately important junction and traffic centre where the branch to Keswick and Workington diverged about a mile south of the station while three miles further on the line to Appleby diverged at Eden Valley Junction. In the 1959 summer timetable ten trains in each direction were advertised on Mondays to Fridays on the former line, but nearly all would have been formed of diesel units, the Keswick route being one of the very first in Great Britain to be favoured with diesel traction, in 1955. The line to Appleby was entirely steam operated until February 1958 when diesel units took over most passenger services on this spectacular cross-Pennine route which connected Darlington and Barnard Castle with the eastern fringe of the Lake District. It is unfortunate that the introduction of more economical diesel trains on these essentially rural lines failed to save either from closure. The Appleby line closed in early 1962 while the Workington route was closed west of Keswick during the Beeching era, but a stub remained open as far as there until 1972. In this illustration another un-rebuilt, un-named 'Patriot' is seen, this time No.45544, which is depicted pulling away from Penrith station with an Edinburgh to Manchester working on 15th August 1959. *Bob Leslie / Peter Robinson collection*

Opposite bottom: The lofty signal box at the north end of Penrith station appears to have been specially designed to ensure the signalman's view was not obstructed by the adjacent road bridge. Stanier Class 5MT No.45371 is seen passing through the station with a southbound goods train on 24th July 1963. *Rodney Lissenden*

Above: The 'Royal Scot' Class 7P 4-6-0s were a familiar sight on the West Coast Main Line for decades but the rapid introduction of diesels on the route in the early 1960s consigned many to the scrap yards and by the end of 1964 only five examples were active. The final survivor was No.46115 *Scots Guardsman* which remained in use on a variety of duties, working from Carlisle (Kingmoor) shed, until December 1965. On 20th October it was noted on the 4.45pm Glasgow (St.Enoch) to Carlisle stopping train but was observed receiving attention in Kingmoor repair shop on 5th November. In this portrait it is leaving the up loop at Plumpton with the 3.15pm Carlisle yard to Crewe Basford Hall goods after being overtaken by the 12.20pm Perth to London Euston passenger train. This photograph was taken in October 1965 and this was the last time the photographer saw a 'Royal Scot' in BR active service. The line southwards from Carlisle climbs virtually all the way to Shap summit but there are one or two level sections, the longest of these being a two miles-long length at Plumpton, so that would have been to the crew's advantage as they left the loop with a heavy train. *Peter Robinson*

During the dying days of BR steam most locomotives were in deplorable external condition, covered with thick grime, so the appearance of a clean locomotive was always a bonus for photographers. Stanier Class 5MT No.45258, seen here passing Southwaite with a Carlisle to Willesden perishable freight working, had just been released from Cowlairs Works, Glasgow, following overhaul and was looking quite presentable to say the least. Note the milk tank wagons immediately behind the locomotive. The loops at Southwaite were the first refuge out of Carlisle on the ascent of Shap; there used to be a station at this location but it was closed from 7th April 1952. This shot was taken in October 1966. *Peter Robinson*

Compared to the totals of 842 'Black Fives' and 645 Fowler/Stanier 2-6-4Ts produced, the Class 6P/5F 2-6-0s introduced in 1933 comprised a mere 40 locomotives and was a very small class numerically. These engines were designed by Stanier, this being his first design of main line locomotives for the LMS after his arrival from Swindon. They were a modified version of the Hughes/Fowler 'Crabs' and had a taper boiler and exerted almost the same tractive effort: the engines were built at Crewe between October 1933 and March 1934. In the early 1960s half of the class were allocated to either Crewe North or Crewe South sheds which suggests that they would have been a frequent sight working over the WCML to Carlisle but, strangely, very few pictures of them were submitted for publication in this album. No.42954, seen here passing the site of Wreay station with a Carlisle to Crewe express freight, spent some time at Crewe North in the 1950s but was actually allocated to Springs Branch (Wigan) shed when this photograph was taken in July 1965. Wreay station had been closed for more than 20 years when this shot was taken: it was a wartime casualty and the last trains called in August 1943. *Peter Robinson*

Carlisle – undoubtedly one of Great Britain's most fascinating railway centres. The first line opened in the city was the Newcastle & Carlisle Railway (N&C) which dated from 19th July 1836 while the Maryport & Carlisle (M&C), which opened to a station in Crown Street in 1843, was not far behind. Three years later the London & North Western (LNW) and Caledonian railways (CR) obtained powers to build a station for the emerging West Coast Main Line but the M&C was obstructive and the LNW was forced to obtain a court order to enable construction of Carlisle Citadel station to continue, the new station eventually opening on 1st September 1847. The station took its name from the nearby Citadel law courts which were completed in 1811. There was a series of disagreements between the various companies, principally due to the dictatorial attitude of the LNW and CR, and tolerable relations were not really achieved until the Carlisle Station Joint Committee was formed by Act of Parliament in 1861. By the time the Midland Railway's epic Settle & Carlisle route reached the city in 1876 there were no fewer than seven companies operating into the station. Originally it consisted of one main platform which was hopelessly inadequate, so the Joint Committee embarked on a £380,000 scheme to enlarge the premises, the principal feature being extensive remodelling and a new island platform. A glazed roof was built at the same time and the enlarged area of the station was brought into use on 4th July 1880. The attractive station frontage was designed by Sir William Tite in the Tudor style and incorporated the Royal arms of the various companies who contributed to the construction costs. The station's interior has remained largely unchanged but the original roof suffered years of wartime neglect and was replaced in the 1950s. In this illustration rebuilt 'Patriot' Class 7P 4-6-0 No.45512 *Bunsen* is depicted at the south end of the station on 20th July 1963. *Rodney Lissenden*

During the pre-Grouping era no fewer than seven different companies operated into Citadel station, as previously mentioned, and the range of liveries sported by their locomotives and carriages must have been breathtaking. Latterly, during the twilight of steam a little of this cosmopolitan air was still to be seen and Carlisle was probably the only location in the country where Pacific class locomotives of both the LMS and LNER could be viewed standing side by side in everyday service. On 26th June 1959 at about 4.15pm Gresley Class A3 No.60079 *Bayardo* was waiting to take a train over the Waverley route to Edinburgh whilst standing alongside was Stanier 'Princess Royal' Class No.46210 *Lady Patricia* which was taking water during a station stop with a Birmingham to Glasgow express. By the date of this picture both machines were well into the autumn of their lives, No.60079 being withdrawn in September 1961 while No.46210 was among the first batch of its class to be withdrawn a month later. Ironically, bearing in mind the fierce competition between the LMS and LNER during the 1930s, *Bayardo* spent the last 13 years of its career at Carlisle (Canal) shed while *Lady Patricia* was also a London Midland Region-based locomotive at the time of the photograph. *Noel Machell*

Atmospheric railway. Trails of smoke and steam hang in the air as BR Standard 'Clan' Pacific No.72008 *Clan Macleod* gets under way from a signal check and passes over a bridge across the river Eden about two miles north of Carlisle station. The locomotive was hauling the 11.00am from Carlisle to Glasgow St. Enoch via Dumfries and this picture was taken in foggy conditions in November 1964. In their latter days the 'Clans' were often to be found on relatively lightweight formations, as seen here, and were regular performers on three-coach Settle & Carlisle stopping trains. The bridge on the right was constructed during the Second World War to ease a bottleneck and hasten the movement of equipment required for the war effort. The former GSW route via Dumfries had a very sparse local service at this time consisting of only three up and two down trains along the entire length of the route, though the latter were supplemented by an early morning train from Annan to Glasgow. In addition there were a number of express services, such as 'The Thames Clyde Express', which served only the major stations while overnight passengers from London to Dumfries enjoyed the luxury of being able to alight from 'The Northern Irishman' at 2.48am. On Sundays the local stations were closed and the service restricted to three long distance trains to and from London plus an evening Glasgow to Dumfries and vice versa service. *Peter Robinson*

Snowy Kingmoor. In early November 1965 Carlisle experienced its heaviest snowfall for years and here Ivatt Class 4MT 2-6-0 No.43040 is seen heading for the marshalling yard with a train of vans from Citadel station. The tracks on the right formed a chord that was laid in 1963 to enable freights from the Waverley route to gain access to the new marshalling yard. The other locomotives in the picture on the right are Class 5MT No.44998 and B1 No.61099 which were booked to work freight trains from the yard and were following the van train under permissive block working arrangements. The main line tracks are immediately to the left of the van train. *Peter Robinson*

Train spotting at Carlisle station must have been a frustrating experience because all the goods traffic used a loop line to bypass the station. This avoiding line was authorised by the Carlisle Citadel Act of 1873 in order to segregate passenger and goods traffic which was growing rapidly at that time and causing considerable congestion in the Carlisle area. The Carlisle Goods Traffic Committee, composed of representatives from the LNWR, CR, MR and GSWR, was formed to construct the line which ran from Bog Junction, on a lower level south of Citadel station, to Caldew Junction on the WCML and Willowholme Junction where it converged with the 'Waverley' route to Edinburgh and the Silloth branch. Whilst the avoiding line, which was brought into use in 1877, revolutionised traffic in the area and doubtless eased pressure on Citadel station it did not solve the problem of the multiplicity of goods depots. These had proliferated as the number of railway companies serving the city had increased and generally each had its own depot, but at least Dentonholme depot, opened in 1883, which was strategically situated adjacent to the Bog Junction to Caldew Junction loop line, was shared by three companies. This needless duplication of facilities necessitated much wasteful trip working and it was said that no fewer than eleven yards existed in 1922 and, not surprisingly, all this activity provided employment for a substantial number of Carlisle's workforce. A new marshalling yard was built north of the city in the early 1960s to eliminate the trip working but wagonload traffic was already in decline and the yard soon became something of a white elephant. Unfortunately, on 1st May 1984 a container train became divided on the descent from Penrith and the staff on duty in the power signal box at Carlisle, which supervised movements over a wide area, immediately noticed something was amiss. They decided to divert the runaway section of the train onto the loop line, thus avoiding the main station and, possibly, preventing a catastrophic collision. This section careered along at speed and, unfortunately, collided with a bridge over the river Caldew, near Dentonholme goods depot, causing extensive damage to the track and bridge structure and some containers ended up in the river. The destruction was so severe it was deemed that the rebuilding of the bridge could not be justified financially and the avoiding line was closed. In this photograph BR Standard 'Britannia' Pacific No.70009 *Alfred the Great* is seen heading a southbound freight working at Rome Street junction, on the Carlisle goods avoiding line, and would have reached the WCML at Upperby Junction. The line in the background, partially hidden by foliage, connected the avoiding line with the route along the Cumbrian coast to Workington. Rome Street junction also provided access to Canal Junction (connection closed from 2nd June 1969) and a former North British Railway goods depot so it is possible that this would have been a better location for spotters, but they would have missed out on the more glamorous express passenger locomotives. You can't win them all. *Cumbrian Railways Association*

Another scene on the Carlisle goods avoiding line, this time showing Stanier Class 5MT 4-6-0 No.45210 passing Dentonholme goods depot with the river Caldew just creeping into the picture on the right. The goods line divided for a short distance at this point into two separate double track routes, hence the line veering off to the right which appears at first sight to be an entirely separate line. The goods line usually offered only an endless procession of mundane freight workings and lacked the more impressive locomotive types that could be observed on a daily basis at the station. Consequently, it tended to be ignored by railway photographers and an interesting aspect of Carlisle's railway heritage has, perhaps, not received the coverage it deserved. This picture was taken in the mid-1960s. *Cumbrian Railways Association*

The first few miles of the S&C line north of Settle do not offer many scenic vistas because the line runs through the Stainforth gorge, a spectacular narrow defile which the railway shares with the tumbling waters of the river Ribble. By the time Horton-in-Ribblesdale station (850 feet above sea level) has been reached, the landscape has changed dramatically: it has really opened out and Pen-y-ghent, one of the famous three peaks of this area, is in view. In this picture a northbound goods train, hauled by Stanier Class 5MT 4-6-0 No.45100, passes the tiny signal box and cattle pens at Horton on 23rd May 1959. The station here is just over half way up the 15 miles long climb from Settle Junction, universally known as the 'Long Drag', so No.45100's fireman would have had some hard work to perform before the summit was reached. *Gavin Morrison*

The Settle & Carlisle – the Midland Railway's epic route to Scotland. In 1832 the coal masters of Nottinghamshire heard of the success of moving coal by rail and the Midland Counties Railway was eventually formed, and from this small company grew the Midland Railway (MR). In 1844 an Act was passed authorising a line between Lancaster and Carlisle, this being routed via Oxenholme to appease the people of Kendal who had campaigned for the line to pass near their town. In the following year the North Western Railway Company (NWR) proposed a route from the West Riding up the Lune Valley via Ingleton to connect with the Carlisle line and this received the Royal Assent in 1846. The year 1846 also saw the formation of the London & North Western Railway (LNWR), a development that was to greatly affect the MR in later years. Robert Stephenson, son of the pioneering George, was asked to advise the NWR on future activity and recommended that the company should shelve the Lune valley line and give priority to reaching Lancaster. Work on the former line had proceeded apace, however, and the contractor was permitted to finish the line as far as Ingleton where there was great rejoicing when it opened in 1849. The line to Lancaster was opened on 1st June 1850 and operation of the route was taken over by the MR two years later. A further development was the construction of a link between Ingleton and Low Gill by the LNWR and inauguration of a passenger service in 1861. The MR's passengers destined for Carlisle were forced to leave their train at Ingleton and trudge across the town to board a LNWR train. Connections were very poor and many passengers had to change trains again at Tebay. James Allport, general manager of the MR, complained that it was 'a very rare thing for me to go down to Carlisle without being turned out twice'. The two giant companies had to come together but the LNWR was in a strong bargaining position and the negotiations foundered and broke up without agreement. But then a new company burst upon the

scene: called the North of England Union Railway, it outlined an ambitious plan for a line connecting Settle with Hawes and Darlington. The MR held meetings with the promoters who offered to withdraw their Bill and it was agreed that the MR would re-introduce the Bill in a modified form. The MR's 'modifications' were quite far reaching and it proposed creating a new route to Carlisle through the Pennines and, moreover, a line that was designed for express trains, not slow local services. The Bill was re-introduced on 16th July 1866 with strong opposition from the MR's rivals, the LNWR, but it received the Royal Assent. The year 1866 saw rapid expansion of the MR on all fronts but the directors had full confidence in the Settle & Carlisle scheme and John Crossley, the company's chief engineer who had been on the point of retiring, was persuaded to stay on as resident engineer. So, the MR's dream of opening its own route to Scotland was at last within its grasp and, remarkably, it was at this point the LNWR suddenly became conciliatory and negotiations about the joint use of the Lancaster to Carlisle line commenced. In November 1868 agreement between the two companies was reached, a condition being that the MR would seek abandonment of the 1866 Bill. Many parliamentarians, however, were dismayed by the number of new railway schemes being proposed and subsequently abandoned and wanted to discourage further speculative proposals, and the MR's Bill for abandonment was rejected. Work on the S&C line had been suspended in January 1868, so the MR's construction committee was hastily re-formed and four tenders invited for various sections of the route plus a fifth for the Hawes branch. Early in 1870 navvies were recruited and construction work began in earnest. Subsequent generations have come to regard Parliament's decision to turn down the abandonment Bill as one of the most enlightened they ever made! *Gavin Morrison*

Above: Photographed on the same day as the previous picture, a Class 4F 0-6-0, No.44009, lays a smokescreen across the fells as it toils up the 1 in 100 gradient towards Blea Moor with a goods train which includes in its consist two BR Standard General Utility vans marshalled immediately behind the locomotive. Horton-in-Ribblesdale station is just visible towards the rear of the train. This locomotive was one of a class of 192 machines that were Fowler's final development of the Midland Railway's long line of 0-6-0 goods engines, the ancestry of which can be traced back to 1888, and this particular locomotive was built at Derby in 1920 and gave good service, lasting until June 1964. This class was later adopted by the LMS as its standard goods engine and 580 were constructed between November 1924 and March 1941. *Gavin Morrison*

High summer on the Settle and Carlisle. The incessant rain lashes down as a Locomotive Club of Great Britain rail tour pauses, as scheduled, for a supposed photographic stop at Ribblehead station on 4th June 1966. A brace of Stanier 'Jubilee' 4-6-0s, Nos.45593 *Kolhapur* and 45596 *Bahamas,* was provided as motive power, an appropriate choice bearing in mind the class's very long association with the route. The participants doubtless grumbled about the diabolical weather and had further cause to complain when damage to overhead wires south of Crewe resulted in a very late arrival in the Capital. Annual rainfall totals at Ribblehead regularly exceed 70 inches, one of the wettest years being 1954 when an unprecedented 109½ inches fell. The Meteorological Office recognised the unpredictable climatic conditions at Ribblehead station, the premises doubling as a weather station charged with sending hourly reports to headquarters. *Rail Photoprints*

An unidentified BR Standard Class 9F 2-10-0, powering a northbound goods train, was captured crossing the iconic Ribblehead viaduct, sometimes known as Batty Moss, on a sunny 14th October 1966. Ribblehead is the longest on the S&C line and is, perhaps, the best known of the route's many impressive viaducts. It is 440 yards-long, consists of 24 arches and is 104 feet above ground at its highest point; some of the piers are especially strengthened, as seen here. One of the most protracted tasks for the builders was to locate sound bases for the piers and shafts were sunk through soft ground to underlying rock, some of the piers being rooted 25 feet below the surface of the moor. Work began on the viaduct in October 1870 and took five years to complete, principally due to the appalling Pennine weather. The viaduct's piers were erected using a wooden framework and sometimes the velocity of the wind made it unsafe for men to continue work. During the peak of the construction work, as many as 2,000 navvies were employed, housed in rudimentary wooden huts in shanty towns such as Batty Wife Hole, a name derived from a pothole in the area. Other shanty towns, crudely built on the bare moorland, had equally colourful names such as Sebastopol, Belgravia and Salt Lake City. These places were served by local traders, including farmers who drove cows into the area on the hoof, beef apparently being the staple diet of many navvies. Businesses boomed during the building work, perhaps none more so than the local brewers, but bare fist fights, fuelled by excessive drinking, were a common occurrence among the navvies. The MR encouraged the moderating influence of the Bible and appointed a scripture reader who initially preached in the open air and later held indoor services in one of the huts. Many of the the navvies were Irish while others came from all over Great Britain, attracted by the high wages, but their loyalty was certainly suspect because during the autumn many left to help with the harvest. Sadly, almost a hundred navvies perished during the construction work at Ribblehead as a result of disease, accidents or simply the damp, inhospitable climate and they were laid to rest in the churchyard at Chapel-le-Dale, two miles from Ribblehead. *John Goss*

Alberta's swan song. A small number of Stanier 'Jubilee' Class 6P5F 4-6-0s were retained at the Eastern Region's Holbeck shed, Leeds, long after the last members of the class had been disposed of by the London Midland Region and were used on various Saturdays only passenger trains over the S&C line during 1967. Their Indian summer could not last for ever, however, and steam traction took its final bow in the Leeds area during the weekend of 30th September/1st October 1967. To commemorate this sad occasion on 30th September No.45593 *Kolhapur* was assigned to the 2.40pm Leeds to Heysham parcels train while No.45562 *Alberta* had a more strenuous duty working the 1.30pm Hunslet to Carlisle freight over the S&C. In addition to its normal consist the latter train also conveyed a brake van immediately behind the locomotive conveying members of the Railway Correspondence & Travel Society's West Riding branch. *Alberta*'s crew clearly entered into the spirit of the occasion and Settle Junction was reportedly passed at 60 mph, somewhat over the limit for the short wheelbase vehicles forming the train. This exertion winded No.45562 with the result that speed had dropped to 12mph by the time Helwith Bridge was reached. Steady progress was made as far as Blea Moor where *Alberta* was photographed on the final stage of the climb, the summit being less than a mile distant in Blea Moor tunnel. The signal box at this location, which is in a particularly isolated and lonely spot, is just discernible adjacent to the cluster of buildings on the left. Originally, the box was on the northbound side of the line but was re-located in 1941 when the old lie-by sidings were replaced by loops, presumably to aid the movement of goods during the Second World War. *John Goss*

The workmanship involved in constructing the splendid stone viaducts along the S&C line is easy to appreciate but Blea Moor tunnel is the most widely acclaimed of the route's civil engineering works, despite the only visible features being the two cavernous portals and ventilation shafts. The statistics speak for themselves: the tunnel is 2,629 yards long, has three ventilation shafts of ten feet diameter, the deepest of which has a depth of 390 feet from moor to rail level, and the tunnel's maximum depth is 500 feet below the top of the moor. Bored between 1870 and 1875 at a cost of £45 per yard, dynamite was the principal explosive used, imported by the MR at a cost of £200 per ton, while the navvies worked by candlelight for which the MR had to foot a bill of £50 per month. The tunnel is actually 400 yards longer than that originally envisaged in order to avoid very deep cuttings at the southern end which may have been a perpetual threat to traffic due to landslips. A particularly fascinating feature, never seen by ordinary mortals, is 'The Donkey Hole' a rocky cavity at the southern end used by engineers and navvies during construction. The massive bulk of the moor dominates the background in this portrait of BR Standard 'Britannia' Pacific No.70004 *William Shakespeare* threading Dentdale with the 9.47am Brindle Heath (Manchester) to Carlisle goods on 31st July 1967. Note the smoke-belching entrance to the tunnel in the background. *John Goss*

While the few roads in the area generally run along the bottom of the dales, the S&C line runs along ledges on the side of the fells or on lofty viaducts, as seen here. In this shot Class 5MT 4-6-0 No.44824 rides high above the valley floor as it crosses Arten Gill viaduct with a southbound freight on 4th February 1967. It must have been the photographer's lucky day as the train's appearance seems to have coincided with a welcome patch of sunlight. Built over a tumbling beck from which it takes its name, Arten Gill viaduct was built of a local stone known as Dent or Black marble. This magnificent structure, completed in 1875, is 220 yards long, 117 feet high and consists of eleven spans. *John Goss*

In the mid-1960s the local service along the S&C was meagre, reflecting the scattered rural community it served, and consisted of two stopping trains in each direction along the entire length of the route, plus one or two short workings between Appleby and Carlisle. By this time the principal expresses had been diesel-hauled for some time but the stopping trains remained steam-worked for much longer and gave enthusiasts the opportunity of a steam-hauled ride along this legendary route. Dent, the highest main line station in England, is the location of this photograph which dates from the mid-1960s and depicts BR Standard 'Britannia' Pacific No.70029 *Shooting Star*. The opening of Dent station was delayed while the MR deliberated over its location, various options being considered until the present site was decided upon, and the premises opened in 1877. The station is about four miles from (and 500 feet above) the village it is purported to serve so is likely to have been used by only the most determined traveller. *Tim Stephens*

Utter frustration. A multitude of enthusiasts made the long trek from the south of England and Midlands to see the last Stanier 'Jubilees' in action, the locomotives reportedly being the pride and joy of the Leeds area Motive Power Superintendent who kept them in traffic for as long as possible, thus earning the eternal gratitude of many. The opportunities to see the three remaining locomotives, Nos.45562 *Alberta*, 45593 *Kolhapur* and 45697 *Achilles* were limited and sometimes the atrocious Pennine weather ruined any possibility of a decent action shot. One particularly wretched day that will always be remembered by steam devotees was 29th July 1967 when it poured with rain for most of the day, frustrating the efforts of photographers anxious to obtain that elusive 'master shot'. The undoubted scenic beauties of the valley in the background, through which the Clough river flows, are concealed by the driving rain in this photograph of *Kolhapur* taking water on Garsdale troughs. There is a level stretch of track here, which fortuitously coincides with the half-way point between Leeds and Carlisle, and the MR installed the troughs at this ideal location in 1907. A 43,000-gallon storage tank was provided to collect water drained off the fells. Note the milepost indicating the distance of 256 miles from St. Pancras. *John Goss*

The original Act of Parliament authorising the S&C line included a six miles-long branch from Garsdale (then known as 'Hawes Junction') to Hawes where it made an end-on connection with the North Eastern Railway's route to Leyburn and Northallerton. The single track branch, which was notable for some substantial civil engineering works, opened on 1st October 1878, some time after the inauguration of services along the S&C line that had been given priority. The growth of bus services and private motoring sealed the fate of this rural route, which served a very sparsely populated area, and the last train through from Garsdale to Northallerton ran on 24th April 1954. The short branch to Hawes lasted a little longer, however, the final train from Hawes being the 4.25pm to Hellifield on 14th March 1959 hauled by Stanier Class 4MT 2-6-4T No.42492. This train was universally known to S&C railwaymen as the 'Bonnyface', reputedly because it conveyed permanent way staff returning home in a happy frame of mind at the end of their working day, but nobody is really sure of the origin of this intriguing piece of Dales folklore. Here, the fireman of sister engine No.42491, from Hellifield shed, provides a cheerful grin for the photographer as he awaits departure from the loop platform with a branch train. Note the tiny ticket office, oil lamps and flower bed in the foreground indicating that the station was still staffed at the time of the picture which was presumably taken in the late 1950s. *Cumbrian Railways Association*

Garsdale – an isolated railway community. Photographed on a glorious late summer day, the 'North Eastern Rail Tour', with 'Princess Coronation' Class 8P Pacific No.46238 *City of Carlisle* in charge, waits in the down platform while the participants explore Garsdale station. No.46238 was working one of the first legs of a five days-long extended tour of lines in the north of England and this picture was taken on 27th September 1963. Garsdale was the only passenger junction station on the S&C line (the connection at Appleby was never regularly used for passenger trains) and branch services to Hawes and Northallerton used the loop platform on the right of the shot. In MR days this was a very busy location due to the large number of pilot locomotives that were detached from both northbound and southbound trains, and a stockaded turntable was installed to turn them. Originally known as 'Hawes Junction' the station's name was changed to Garsdale in 1932, and if the MR's plans had come to fruition there would have been substantial development here consisting of 30 houses and a locomotive shed large enough to accommodate 24 engines. These ideas were substantially scaled down, however, and only a few houses were actually constructed while a single road engine shed was provided. Interestingly, the stone built dwellings were a trifle out of place in the dales, being modelled on urban back-to-back housing that typified many northern cities. The magnificent water-tank house at Garsdale (not in the picture) served for many years as a community centre and boasted a piano and small stage but, regrettably, this substantial building was demolished in 1971. This illustration shows rail tour participants wandering around, no doubt admiring the lovely scenery including Baugh Fell and Rise Hill which attain the heights of 2,216 and 1,825 feet above sea level respectively. The tour passengers may not have been so impressed with the somewhat basic facilities at Garsdale, compared to other S&C stations, and *bona fide* passengers waiting at this windswept location must have rued the day when the loop platform canopies were removed. *Cumbrian Railways Association*

The section of line between Garsdale station and Ais Gill summit is relatively level, but also one of the bleakest and most exposed on the entire route, with bare and inhospitable moorland stretching as far as the eye can see. The line crosses a watershed from where becks flow into the river Lune, which reaches the sea near Lancaster, and river Ure, a tributary of the river Ouse, which flows into the Humber estuary. The river Eden, which reaches the Solway Firth near Carlisle, has its source close to Ais Gill summit and the railway runs along the valley of the river for much of the way to Carlisle. Even in the summer the S&C line is plagued by dull and misty conditions, as seen here as Stanier 'Jubilee' Class 6P5F No.45593 *Kolhapur* heads across Lunds viaduct with the 9.20am St. Pancras to Glasgow relief on 19th August 1967. On a clear day the view down Wensleydale towards Hawes is memorable but on the day of this photograph low cloud and mist conspired to obscure the beauty of the fells. The viaduct, which takes its name from the nearby hamlet of Lunds, spans a ravine from where much stone was quarried to build the viaduct and other structures. Constructed in 1874, the five-arch Lunds viaduct is 103 yards-long and 63 feet high.
John Goss

Ais Gill summit is marked by the cottages on the horizon and in this illustration BR Standard Class 9F No.92096 is within sight of the summit and end of the long, relentless climb from Appleby. The locomotive was working a Long Meg to Widnes anhydrite train, formed of distinctive hopper mineral wagons, and this picture was taken on a stormy February day in 1966. The lonely Moorcock Inn to Kirkby Stephen road can be seen on the left of the line. There was some sort of cafe at Ais Gill cottages but it rarely seemed to be open and, perhaps, its opening times were confined to warm, dry summer days in which case they would have been severely limited. *Peter Robinson*

The S&C line is carried on a shelf high above Mallerstang Common and this is one of the most inaccessible stretches of the route. In this evocative picture smoke and steam billow back along the train as 'Britannia' Pacific No.70010 *Owen Glendower* grapples with the 1 in 100 gradient that applies at this point. Enginemen aboard locomotives that were steaming badly were no doubt grateful in times gone by for a brief section just beyond Birkett tunnel where the gradient eased to 1 in 330. The 'Britannia' was working a special train run on 5th February 1967 for Welsh rugby fans returning home to Cardiff following an International game with Scotland in Edinburgh. Altogether eight special trains were provided for Welsh supporters, four of which were steam hauled by 'Britannia' Pacifics. It was, perhaps, surprising that spare diesel locomotives were apparently not available on a Sunday. The signal box just visible in the background is Mallerstang but on the day of this picture it was presumably 'switched out', hence all of the signals are in the 'off' position. Latterly, it was said that the box was only open at night, a busy time for freight traffic, and a night shift at this lonely outpost must have been quite an experience. The box had no road access and could only be reached by trudging across fields, hardly an inviting prospect on a wild Pennine night. *John Goss*

Alberta takes her final bow on the S&C. During the summer of 1967 Holbeck shed's trio of 'Jubilee' Class 4-6-0s made regular sorties over the Settle line, as previously mentioned, giving much pleasure to many enthusiasts travelling on the trains and photographing from the lineside. No.45697 *Achilles* was taken out of traffic in September while sister engine No.45593 *Kolhapur* survived only a month longer. This left No.45562 *Alberta* as the sole remaining 'Jubilee' and final LMS-designed express passenger locomotive in traffic, the last of a long and illustrious breed. On 7th October No.45562 powered 'The South Yorkshireman' rail tour over the S&C line and, incredibly, bearing in mind the route's reputation among photographers, the train passed Smardale just at the right time during a period of strong autumn sunshine which produced a marvellous glint on the side of the train. This was probably the last time a 'Jubilee' worked over the line, a memorable historical event that will be forever etched in the memories of those hardy, enterprising and patient folk who were present. By the date of this picture Holbeck shed had been officially closed to steam traction and No.45562 spent the last few weeks of its BR service at Normanton. On 25th October *Alberta* powered the 3.05pm Leeds City to Patricroft parcels train and three days later was observed on Normanton shed. It was apparently considered for private preservation but its driving wheel tyres were very thin and this sealed its fate, and No.45562 unfortunately went for scrap. *John Goss*

Southbound at Crosby Garrett. Class 4F 0-6-0 No.44119 heads southwards with a long goods train in tow on 19th July 1958 and is about to enter Crosby Garrett tunnel, which is 181 yards long and 269 miles from St. Pancras. There is a brief respite here in the 1 in 100/165 gradient that applies most of the way from Ormside, but the 1 in 100 incline resumes in earnest at the south end of the tunnel and continues almost the rest of the way to Ais Gill, so No.44119's fireman would have had his work cut out. The station here served an isolated Pennine village which was dominated by the six-arch viaduct that took the line across a small ravine but, presumably, patronage wasn't sufficient to justify its retention and it was closed from 6th October 1952. The signal box at this location remained open long after the station was shut and initial closure occurred on 12th April 1965, but it remained operative until 1967.
Bob Leslie/Peter Robinson collection

In the 1960s technology was not as advanced as it is today and BR special traffic and engineering works arrangements were distributed in printed notices normally despatched by train from headquarters and divisional offices. Every signalman on the system needed this information but communicating with staff at Crosby Garrett was difficult because latterly the box was only open 'as required' so very often there was nobody on hand to receive the vital notices. Not to be defeated by such a problem, BR ingeniously solved this difficulty by providing an 'official' special, waterproof storage receptacle, otherwise known as a dustbin. The 8.35am Carlisle to Skipton diesel unit made a special stop at Crosby Garrett signal box and in this photograph the guard is seen depositing a bundle of paperwork before rejoining the train. This was simply the cheapest and most effective means of delivering the weekly notices which was universally known to railway enthusiasts travelling on the train as the Crosby Garrett 'dustbin stop'.
John Goss

A view from the footbridge of Appleby station with Stanier Class 5MT No.44884, which was in charge of a southbound freight train, taking water; this photograph was taken in the mid-1960s. Whilst the station's name, prominently displayed in whitewashed stone beside the southbound platform, left passengers in no doubt regarding the station's identity, more knowledgeable folk would have known that Appleby was the only station on the route originally favoured with a footbridge. In addition, the main station building was constructed of brick with stone dressings whereas most other structures on the line were built of local stone. The station is also noted for a very attractive and elaborate glass screen between the booking hall and platform. Church bells reputedly rang out in the town when the Act of Parliament authorising the line was passed, and the MR certainly provided excellent facilities for the townsfolk: there was a substantial goods shed and cattle pens while from the operational aspect there were two signal boxes and a massive tank house, visible above the train, to ensure locomotives were always able to replenish their supply. The signal box just discernible beyond the starting signal in this shot was known as Appleby West and was brought into use in 1890 and closed on 14th October 1973. *John Goss*

Seen from above the southern portal of Culgaith tunnel on 19th August 1967, a northbound van train hauled by Stanier Class 5MT No.44727, is about to plunge into the 661 yards-long bore. The signal box, which controlled a level crossing, is just discernible through the locomotive's exhaust trail while Culgaith station's northbound platform is also visible. The station was situated in a peaceful location on the hillside between river Eden and the village, the tranquillity being only occasionally disturbed by passing motorists, farm tractors and, of course, the occasional train. The distant, conical shaped peaks of Knock Pike and Dufton Pike can just be made out through the mist, the latter rising to a height of 1,578 feet above sea level. It is often said that the minor stations on the S&C line were of a uniform, standard design but Culgaith was not opened until 1880 and is in a different architectural style to the others. The level crossing is one of only two on the line, the other being at Low House near Armathwaite. *John Goss*

A shaft of sunlight breaks through a leaden sky and beautifully illuminates Class 4F 0-6-0 No.43896 which is seen shunting anhydrite wagons at Langwathby on 3rd November 1956. Note the dainty lower quadrant signal on the left of the picture and cattle pens in the foreground on the right. The mineral anhydrite originated from a mine at Long Meg, near Lazonby, where the Long Meg Plaster and Mineral Co. Ltd. commenced operations in the 1890s, and it subsequently became one of the major sources of originating traffic on the S&C route. *Bob Leslie / Peter Robinson collection*

The relief 'Thames-Clyde Express', with BR Standard 'Britannia' Pacific No.70016 *Ariel* in charge, is seen between Lazonby and Armathwaite on 22nd July 1967, a brilliantly sunny day. *Ariel,* which was out-shopped from Crewe works in June 1951, was allocated to Plymouth (Laira) shed for use on crack Paddington expresses, but later moved to Cardiff (Canton) where it was based for a number of years. In 1961 No.70016 was 'surplus to requirements' on the Western Region and was transferred to the LMR, working at various periods from Manchester (Longsight) and Birmingham (Aston) sheds before being based at Carlisle (Kingmoor) where many 'Britannias' were allocated for the last years of their BR service. *John Goss*

Stanier Class 6P/5F 'Jubilee' No.45593 *Kolhapur* is depicted in the splendid setting of the Eden valley, the railway having largely followed the river all the way from its source near Ais Gill summit. The more northerly sections of the S&C route were often neglected by photographers but some attractive locations were available, such as this section of line between Lazonby and Armathwaite. The Pennine range forms a distant backdrop as No.45593 heads towards Carlisle with the 10.17am Leeds to Glasgow also on 22nd July 1967. This summer Saturday train actually commenced its journey at Birmingham (New Street) at 6.40am, ran between 15th July and 26th August, and conveyed through carriages to Glasgow (Central). Engines were changed at Carlisle and, despite the reduction in steam servicing facilities on the Scottish Region following its abandonment of steam traction, a 'Britannia' often took over for the rest of the run to Glasgow. What better day out could a steam enthusiast ask for than being hauled by two named locomotives in succession on the same train? *John Goss*

Commencing on 7th March 1960 seven diagrams for 2,000hp English Electric diesel locomotives were introduced to cover some passenger and freight workings between Newcastle-upon-Tyne and Edinburgh, thus displacing Gresley Pacifics which were transferred to Holbeck shed (Leeds). This was a remarkable development at the former MR shed and the first two arrivals were reportedly Nos.60038 *Firdaussi* and 60077 *The White Knight* which made their appearance during the same month; a further four Class A3s followed in April. During the first week of June the Class A3s started work over the S&C line, initially confined to powering the 'Thames-Clyde Express' in both directions between Leeds and Glasgow, and it was reported that Nos.60038/88/92 had appeared up to 11th June. The A3s were apparently in good condition and the Holbeck crews were said to be delighted with the performance of their unaccustomed motive power. The Pacifics later took over haulage of other expresses between the two cities and a total of nine locomotives was based at the Leeds depot. In this portrait a smartly turned out No.60082 *Neil Gow* passes Baron Wood siding on 20th August 1960 with the down 'Thames-Clyde Express'. A private siding was originally provided there for the Ley family of Lazonby Hall who owned extensive forests in the vicinity and manufactured pit props which were transported from the siding during the First World War. It appears that limited use was made of the facility and the siding was closed in 1951 and the main line connection severed. *Bob Leslie / Peter Robinson collection*

An outrageously expensive trip. BR decided to cash-in on the demise of steam traction by running a 'Farewell to Steam' rail tour on 11th August 1968 but took the fun out of it by charging an exorbitant fifteen guineas, a huge sum at the time, for a 'souvenir' ticket which ensured that only the better off would be able to participate. Consequently, the considerable historical significance of this commemorative special, which was advertised as the last ever on BR tracks, has been lost and it will always be remembered as the 'Fifteen Guinea Special'. Appropriately the train, which started in Liverpool, travelled along the route of the historic Liverpool and Manchester Railway before BR Standard 'Britannia' Pacific No.70013 *Oliver Cromwell* took over for a run to Carlisle via Blackburn and Hellifield. The return journey was entrusted to a pair of 'Black Fives', Nos.44781 and 44871, which are depicted in full cry, in glorious afternoon sunshine, near Armathwaite; part of the parapet of the viaduct can just be discerned. Note that BR could not even be bothered to assemble a uniform rake of either maroon or blue and grey coaching stock. One wonders how passengers who had stumped up fifteen guineas to travel on the supposed 'last' steam train reacted some years later when BR's steam ban was lifted and such tours became commonplace. *Peter Robinson*

A mid summer's day at Armathwaite. A brace of Class 4F 0-6-0s, Nos.44326 and 43863, approach Armathwaite station with a short engineer's train on 10th June 1956. Part of Armathwaite's gently curving viaduct is visible; this graceful 176 yards-long structure was built entirely of stone between 1871 and 1874. It has nine spans of 44ft. 7in. and stands 80 feet above the valley.
Bob Leslie / Peter Robinson collection

An eleven-coach Glasgow (St. Enoch) to Leeds (City) express hurries through Armathwaite on 5th July 1958; motive power is provided by Stanier Class 7P 4-6-0 No.46103 *Royal Scots Fusilier* from Holbeck shed. Locomotives of this class and 'Jubilees' monopolised the Anglo-Scottish expresses until the arrival of the Gresley A3s in June 1960. When the line was built the MR minimised the use of facing points and the only location at which these were originally installed was Appleby, where their use was unavoidable. Note that access to the goods yard was by trailing points only from both main running lines and this layout was repeated at many locations on the line. The roof of Armathwaite's signal box is just visible above the roof of the first vehicle. The compact goods yard was closed from 6th April 1964.
Bob Leslie / Peter Robinson collection

Class 4F 0-6-0 No.44007, heading a southbound mixed goods train, lays a magnificent smokescreen across the Cumberland countryside; it was photographed at Eden Brows, between Cotehill and Armathwaite, on 3rd May 1958. The locomotive is working hard at this point up a 1 in 132 gradient but a few yards further on a minor summit is reached where No.44007 would have been able to take a short downhill 'breather' towards Armathwaite station. Between there and Appleby the line is undulating in nature but once Appleby has been passed the steep gradients begin in earnest and much sterner work is required. *Bob Leslie / Peter Robinson collection*

During the early 1960s Leeds (Holbeck) shed had a modest allocation of three BR Standard 'Britannia' Pacifics, including No.70054 *Dornoch Firth* which is seen here heading southbound with 'The Waverley' Anglo-Scottish express near Cotehill on 18th March 1961. This train served places on the erstwhile Waverley route between Edinburgh and Carlisle, and in the 1959/60 winter timetable it was scheduled to leave Edinburgh at 10.05am and arrive in London (St. Pancras) at 8.00pm. In the opposite direction it left London at 9.15am and was advertised to arrive in Edinburgh at 6.53pm. *Bob Leslie / Peter Robinson collection*

The southbound 'Thames-Clyde Express', with Gresley Class A3 Pacific No.60036 *Columbo* at its head, gets into its stride past Cotehill after departure from Carlisle; this shot was taken on 3rd April 1961. Regrettably, the reign of the A3s on the Anglo-Scottish expresses over the S&C line was cut short by the introduction of BR/Sulzer Type 4 diesel locomotives from 12th June 1961. They took over haulage of the train seen here from that date, while three weeks later 'The Waverley' also succumbed to diesel operation and many of Holbeck's A3s were transferred to other sheds in the Leeds area. Despite these developments Class A3 locomotives were sometimes 'borrowed' and continued to appear on the S&C line on seasonal and relief trains, particularly No.60038 *Firdaussi* which remained at Holbeck for some time after its sister engines had gone. *ARPT*

Photographed in superb, low winter lighting conditions the 'Thames-Clyde Express' is seen again, this time passing Durran Hill, just outside Carlisle, in January 1961. Motive power is provided by a rather grimy Class A3 Pacific, No.60072 *Sunstar*, which is prominently displaying a headboard. The MR laid extensive sidings at this location and built a substantial engine shed plus a small wagon repair depot. *ARPT*

Towards the end of 1844 the Leeds & Bradford Railway was planning a line northwards to Skipton and the Lancaster & Carlisle (L&CR) was about to start building, but a large area of untapped country still remained between Skipton and Lancaster. On 25th February 1845 the inhabitants of Settle met at the 'Golden Lion' public house to declare their support for the North Western Railway (NWR) which was later universally known as the 'Little North Western' to differentiate it from its big brother. The NWR proposed a line from Skipton through Ingleton to Low Gill, five miles south of Tebay, where connection would be made with the L&CR. There was also to be a branch to Lancaster which would diverge from the main line at Clapham. The NWR received the Royal Assent on 26th June 1846 and on New Year's Eve of that year the first sod was dug at Cleatop, two miles from Settle, by a local dignitary who, it is recorded, had considerable difficulty performing the task due to the frozen ground. The company pressed ahead with construction but 1846 proved to be a year of economic difficulties and the NWR was later forced to make economies. In February 1848 Robert Stephenson was asked to advise on the value of the proposed works and recommended immediate construction of the Lancaster branch in preference to the main line to Low Gill, stating that a considerable financial saving could be achieved on building costs. Work on the main line was largely complete as far as Ingleton and it was decided to finish the line at that point; it was formally opened in 1849. The route to Lancaster was opened in stages, from Skipton to Clapham on 30th July 1849 and the section from Lancaster Green Ayre to Wennington four months later: the route was eventually opened throughout on 1st June 1850. In this picture Stanier Class 5MT No.44877 is seen at Eldroth, between Giggleswick and Clapham, hauling a relief Leeds (City) to Morecambe (Promenade) train on a bright and sunny Whit Monday, 3rd June 1963. Whilst Scarborough was probably a more popular destination for most citizens of West Yorkshire towns the photographer comments that many scheduled Leeds/Bradford to Morecambe trains were especially strengthened and reliefs provided as seen here. No.44877 was only six minutes behind the advertised main train which was hauled by sister engine No.45229 of Rose Grove depot. *Noel Machell*

When the line from Clapham to Lancaster was being constructed it was opened in stages, as previously mentioned, and for a very brief period between November 1849 and May 1850 Wennington served as the terminus of trains from Lancaster. In much more recent times this quiet junction station was well known for bursts of activity when trains to and from Leeds required attachments or detachments to be made. Here, Stanier 'Jubilee' Class 4-6-0 No.45573 *Newfoundland* is seen arriving at Wennington with the 2.46pm Morecambe to Leeds train on 12th September 1964, passing Fowler 2-6-4T No.42359 standing on the other track having brought in the portion from Carnforth a few minutes earlier and shunted the coaches into the bay platform on the north side of the station. After stopping in the platform the Morecambe portion would have reversed into the bay and attached the other coaches, the movement being controlled from a ground frame, before resuming its journey to Leeds at 3.17pm. About ten minutes later the 2.50pm Heysham Harbour to Stourton freight would have passed through while No.42359 simmered quietly before departing with the Carnforth portion of the 1.53pm from Leeds, due at 3.38pm. The photographer mentions that this frenetic activity was quite a treat to witness on a glorious September afternoon at a quiet country station. In the early 1960s *Newfoundland* achieved a degree of fame when it starred on a Transacord record featuring a journey over the Settle & Carlisle line. *Noel Machell*

The signal is 'off' for Carnforth as former Midland Railway Class 4F 0-6-0 No.43893 approaches Wennington on 24th September 1964 with a train load of coal presumably destined for the Furness district. This locomotive, which was based at Skipton for its entire BR career, entered traffic in 1919 and lasted in service until May 1965. The tracks on the right were laid during the Second World War as holding loops to cope with increased freight traffic between West Yorkshire and Heysham/Barrow-in-Furness. *Noel Machell*

Travelling in the opposite direction to the train seen in the previous photograph, Hughes/Fowler Class 6P5F 2-6-0 No.42812, powering the 2.50pm Heysham Harbour to Stourton goods, passes Wennington on 21st September 1963. A fair proportion of its payload was containerised traffic that had been offloaded from Belfast ferries. Universally nicknamed 'Crabs' by enthusiasts, No.42812 was one of around half a dozen locomotives of this class based at Lancaster (Green Ayre) shed mainly for hauling freight trains through to the West Riding. The junction for the Morecambe and Carnforth lines is just beyond the overbridge at the rear of the train. *Noel Machell*

The Skipton to Lancaster line crossed the river Lune twice near Crook o' Lune, between Caton and Halton, and here the 12.22pm SO Skipton to Morecambe (Promenade) train, with BR Standard Class 4MT 4-6-0 No.75017 in charge, is depicted crossing the easternmost of the two viaducts some time in the mid-1960s. This attractive route fell victim to the Beeching economies of the 1960s when it was decided to concentrate all traffic from the Leeds/Bradford area to Morecambe on the former joint Furness/Midland Railway line which ran via Arkholme to Carnforth: from there trains proceeded along the West Coast Main Line to either Lancaster or Morecambe. The trackbed between Lancaster and Caton has at least found a new role as a footpath. *Noel Machell*

Halton was the last stop for trains from Skipton before they reached Lancaster (Green Ayre) but the station was located on the south bank of the river Lune while the village was on the north bank. Access from the village to the station was facilitated by a railway-owned toll bridge and the list of tolls contained some delightful anachronisms, such as the 3d. charge for crossing in a horse drawn carriage. The motorcycle parked by the sign tends to suggest that the owner was unable to afford the charge demanded and temporarily abandoned the machine before crossing the bridge. In fact the motor cycle was owned by the porter/signalman who was on duty at Halton station. In this scene Stanier Class 8F No.48067 is captured passing over the crossing with the 12.40pm Heysham (Moss Sidings) to Tees yard train on 24th September 1964. *Noel Machell*

The railway routes covered by this book are, with a few exceptions, famous for the magnificent, unrivalled sight and sound of steam locomotives toiling up fierce gradients amid a barren and desolate moorland landscape. Perhaps the most spectacular line was the Stainmore route across the bleak North Pennines which linked Tebay and Penrith with Barnard Castle, in County Durham. The line was originally built to enable coke from the Durham area to reach the blast furnaces of Barrow and West Cumberland and convey ore in the opposite direction. Trains to and from Barrow-in-Furness were routed from Tebay along the West Coast Main Line as far as Hincaster Junction and then continued to Barrow via Arnside. The first recorded meeting to promote the line took place in Kirkby Stephen in November 1856 and the South Durham & Lancashire Union Railway received the Royal Assent on 13th July 1857. The inaugural mineral trains operated between Tebay and Barnard Castle on 4th July 1861 while the formal opening took place on 7th August. The new line enabled mineral traffic to be transported much more quickly than the circuitous route via Carlisle and Newcastle that had been used hitherto. Passenger traffic was always of secondary importance on the Stainmore line, but latterly attracted the attention of enthusiasts because of the unusual nature of the operation. The Tebay to Kirkby Stephen line lost its regular passenger service from 1st December 1952 but holiday trains from the north-east continued to operate until 1961 and offered a rare chance to travel over the route, albeit for a limited spell during the height of the summer season. Here, Fowler Class 4MT 2-6-4T No.42403, in very spruce condition, is a surprising sight entering Tebay station with an unidentified passenger working some time during the 1950s. Locomotives of this class were not associated with the route and one wonders if this was a special train of some description. No.42403, however, was allocated to Tebay shed for a long period for banking duties on the 'main line' so this picture is something of a mystery. *Cumbrian Railways Association*

Many photographs of trains on the West Coast Main Line have been taken at Tebay over the years but here is a rare glimpse of shunting operations in the 'North Eastern' yard with a nicely cleaned Fowler Class 4F No.44459 prominent. Operations were controlled from Tebay No.3 signal box which is on the right of the shot, and at the time of this photograph the yard was bustling with activity, another locomotive being on the left of the picture. The overcast and dull conditions suggest that rain was imminent. The date of this photograph is not known but No.44459 was a resident of Tebay shed in the early 1950s and perhaps the picture dates from this period. *Cumbrian Railways Association*

By the time this picture was taken on 8th September 1956 the Tebay to Kirkby Stephen East line had been closed to regular passenger traffic for almost four years so one wonders how many passengers appreciated the privilege of being able to travel over such a 'rare' route. Here, hens peck contentedly in the foreground as the 11.20am Blackpool to Newcastle-upon-Tyne train is seen being hurried along near Gaisgill by a pair of BR Standard locomotives, Class 3MT No.82028 and Class 4MT No.76048. Note that, with the exception of the third vehicle, the train is formed of ex-LNER coaching stock from both the Gresley and Thompson eras. *Bob Leslie / Peter Robinson collection*

A blot on the landscape. Following closure of the Stainmore route, BR used the section from Tebay to Ravenstonedale for storage of coal wagons that were surplus to requirements during the summer months. BR's insensitive action in stabling long lines of decrepit wagons in such a beautiful rural area no doubt incensed local folk who were up in arms, and rightly so, and one can imagine letters from angry residents, such as 'outraged of Ravenstonedale', appearing in the local press. One wonders what the 'BR spokesman' would have had to say in response to complaints. In this picture Class WD 2-8-0 No.90157 is seen running tender-first back to its home shed of Tebay after depositing another raft of wagons for the local populace to admire. A week later more exotic motive power, in the shape of former London & North Western Railway 0-8-0 No.49447, was observed near Tebay propelling empty wagons towards Kirkby Stephen. Ravenstonedale station can just be discerned in the background of this scene which was captured on 6th May 1962. *Noel Machell*

The line between Tebay and Ravenstonedale was double track but beyond the latter point it was single and here the 11.20am Blackpool Central to Newcastle-upon-Tyne train is seen leaving behind Ivatt Class 2MT No.46481 and BR Standard Class 4MT No.76049 on 27th July 1957. In the 1960 summer timetable this train was scheduled to stop at Barnard Castle for ten minutes, presumably to take water, and its advertised arrival time in Newcastle was 5.03pm. But, what a journey to remember. *Bob Leslie / Peter Robinson collection*

Photographed on a typically gloomy Pennine day in August 1951, Class J21 No.65047 makes a smoky departure from Kirkby Stephen East with an eastbound train. No.65047 was a real 'old timer' that was built by the North Eastern Railway (NER) at Gateshead as long ago as October 1889 and it lasted in service until December 1954. The old NER locomotives were phased out in the 1950s and replaced by much more modern BR Standard designs, many of the engines being brand new from Darlington works. This was the hub of operations on the Stainmore route where the small, four-road engine shed had an allocation of around a dozen locomotives, many of the duties being piloting or banking heavier trains over this arduous line. *ARPT*

Following the withdrawal of passenger services across the Pennines some sections of the Stainmore route remained open for traffic. The short stub from Eden Valley Junction to Clifton Moor lasted until 6th July 1964 while the Darlington to Middleton-in-Teesdale via Barnard Castle line survived until 5th April 1965 when the final goods train ran, passenger trains having been withdrawn from 30th November 1964. Traffic from Hartley quarry and residual goods traffic from Kirkby Stephen East, which used the connection with the Settle & Carlisle line at Appleby, continued until 31st October 1974 when it was cut back to Flitholm p.w. cabin just south of Warcop. The section from Appleby to Warcop continued to see occasional trains to and from the army depot at Warcop but the last of those is thought to have run in the late 1980s and the line has subsequently been completely abandoned. In this picture Ivatt Class 4MT No.43121 is seen shunting quarry traffic near Merrygill on 19th June 1967. *John Goss*

Opposite: A helping hand. Ivatt Class 2MT No.46470 provides welcome rear-end assistance to Class J21 No.65097 which is in charge of a long train of empty mineral wagons; this picture is thought to have been taken in the early 1950s. The location is unmistakable: the incomparable Belah viaduct which carried the line across the river of the same name. The lonely Belah signal box can just be seen behind the rear locomotive. The viaduct's foundation stone was laid on 25th November 1857 by Henry Pease of Darlington, chairman of the railway company, but construction of this magnificent civil engineering masterpiece really started in earnest on 19th July 1859, the contractors being Gilkes, Wilson & Company of Middlesbrough. The structure's dimensions were impressive: it consisted of 15 wrought iron piers, was 1,047 feet long and a maximum height of 196 feet above the valley bottom. A particularly interesting feature was the way in which the ironwork was tapered, the piers being 50 feet wide at the base but less than half that at the top. Total building costs are reputed to have been £31,630. The viaduct was completely repainted during 1956 which local railwaymen may have viewed as a bad omen because the economics of the line may have already been under scrutiny. Amid considerable controversy, demolition of this remarkable structure commenced on 4th July 1963, just over eighteen months after the last train ran, and was completed with almost indecent haste. A sad end to an iconic railway viaduct. *ARPT*

Above: On the morning of 24th February 1955 BR Standard Class 2MT No.78018, working the 4.20am goods from Kirkby Stephen, became stuck in a massive snowdrift at Bleath Gill, between Barras and Stainmore summit. Teams of permanent way staff from Darlington, Barnard Castle and Kirkby Stephen were summoned to rescue the stranded locomotive and its train and were forced to manually dig out chunks of snow before endeavouring to move the stricken engine. Unfortunately, heat from the locomotive's boiler had melted the snow, only for it to refreeze as ice, and No.78018's motion had frozen solid, defying all attempts to move it. Cotton waste soaked in paraffin was used to thaw out the motion and then steam jets from an assisting locomotive achieved the desired result, and all this work was carried out in bitterly cold conditions with a biting 40mph wind. Staff at the refreshment room at Barnard Castle station worked overtime to provide sustenance to the hungry crews. A team from British Transport Films was on hand to record the rescue and their epic film included spectacular and memorable scenes of an independent snow plough, powered by two locomotives, taking a 'run' at a mountain of hard-packed snow. Their efforts resulted in accolades from the British Film Institute who rated the film 'outstanding' and, perhaps, the fact that the men featured were all BR staff and not actors added to its undoubted realism. *ARPT*

Life for railwaymen working on the Stainmore line must have been demanding, particularly for firemen who had to work really hard on the long climbs up to the summit, but at least they could relax to some degree on the equally long downhill sections. Here, BR Standard Class 2MT No.78017, piloting an unidentified Ivatt Class 4MT 2-6-0 on a westbound freight, begins the descent from Stainmore summit to Kirkby Stephen. The road visible in the background is the A66 cross-Pennine route. *Cumbrian Railways Association*

The tortuous, unrelenting 1 in 59/60 climb from Kirkby Stephen East to Stainmore summit demanded that locomotives worked to their limit and here a combination of two BR Standard 2-6-0 locomotives, Class 3MT No.77004 assisted in the rear by Class 2MT No.78018, exert maximum effort at the approach to Stainmore summit. The pair were powering a Blackpool to Darlington train on 2nd August 1958. One can only imagine the deafening blast as they passed the photographer. *Bob Leslie / Peter Robinson collection*

The crew of BR Standard Class 4MT No.76047 are looking out for the photographer as they breast the summit with a five-coach Blackpool to South Shields holiday train on 26th July 1958. The severity of the gradient can be judged by the manner in which the line drops down towards the overbridge in the background. The local, all-year-round service between Darlington and Penrith was provided by diesel units by this date which had taken over from steam trains on 3rd February 1958. The journey time for the 64¾ miles which separated the two towns was around two hours and there were three return workings on weekdays only. *Bob Leslie / Peter Robinson collection*

Locomotive crews were always eternally grateful when Stainmore signal box came into view because it meant that after miles of stiff gradients, and back breaking work for the fireman, they could take it relatively easy as their train sped downhill. There was a prominent sign marking the summit (hidden by the train) and proclaiming its height of 1,370 feet above sea level. In this shot BR Standard Class 4MT 2-6-0 No.76020 passes the signal box with a holiday train from Blackpool to Darlington on 26th July 1958. *Bob Leslie / Peter Robinson collection*

There is a light dusting of snow on the ground as a stopping train from Penrith to Darlington enters Bowes station some time in the late-1950s: motive power is provided by BR Standard Class 3MT 2-6-2T No.82027. In times gone by the solidly-built station building provided accommodation for the station master and his family. *ARPT*

One on the front...... Belah was not the only viaduct on the Stainmore line to offer a magnificent vista to passengers and the view from Deepdale viaduct was almost as good. Located between Lartington and Bowes, this superb, curving structure was 161 feet high and 740 feet long, and carried the line across a deep, thickly-wooded ravine through which flowed Deepdale Beck. An interesting feature of the viaduct was a catwalk under the decking which gave easy access for maintenance. Here, Ivatt Class 2MT 2-6-0 No.46482, of West Auckland shed, leads a heavy train of County Durham coal across Deepdale viaduct some time in the 1950s. *Cumbrian Railways Association*

......And one on the back. An unidentified Class J21 0-6-0, on the rear of the train seen in the previous shot, was no doubt working 'flat out' in order to give No.46482 a hearty push up the 1 in 81 incline that applies at this point. The gradient steepened immediately to 1 in 69 at the end of the viaduct so let us hope the Class J21 was not 'winded' by its exertion because, after all, there was still a long way to go before the summit was reached. *Cumbrian Railways Association*

A total of 45 BR Standard Class 3MT 2-6-2Ts, Nos.82000 to 82044, was built at Swindon works between April 1952 and August 1955; they were built in two separate batches with a two-year gap, hence the extended delivery period. The locomotives were concentrated on the Southern and Western regions in the late 1950s with the exception of four, Nos.82026 to 82029, which were shared between Darlington and West Hartlepool sheds. These locomotives were frequent visitors to the Stainmore route prior to the introduction of diesel units and here a brace, with No.82028 leading No.82027, are seen between Clifton Moor and Eden Valley Junction; they were working a Saltburn to Penrith train on 1st September 1957. The Stainmore line joined the West Coast Main Line at Eden Valley Junction for the rest of the way to Penrith where trains off the trans-Pennine route normally terminated. *Bob Leslie/Peter Robinson collection*

Apart from the obvious exception of Appleby, all the intermediate stations between Kirkby Stephen and Penrith served small settlements and most were shut between 1952 and 1956, so when the line was closed only Warcop, Appleby East and Clifton Moor were affected. Here, BR Standard Class 2MT 2-6-0 No.78019 is seen leaving Clifton Moor with a southbound train in the 1950s. The building on the right was built as an ornamental private waiting room for Earl Lonsdale who was a resident of nearby Lowther Castle. The line was double track from Eden Valley junction, where it diverged from the West Coast Main Line, but was single south of Clifton Moor as far as Kirkby Stephen. *Cumbrian Railways Association*

During the very early years of railway development some ridiculous schemes were proposed, including the Yorkshire & Glasgow Union Railway's ambitious plan to construct a route from Thirsk to Penrith (Clifton) via Hawes, Kirkby Stephen and Appleby. This would have traversed some of the most desolate and thinly populated areas of the north of England and, almost needless to say, the scheme never progressed beyond the drawing board if, indeed, it got that far. The Eden Valley Railway Company's idea for a line from Kirkby Stephen to Clifton via Appleby was much more worthy of support and attracted sufficient local backers among local entrepreneurs to enable a parliamentary bill to be promoted, and this was passed on 21st May 1858. Construction of this line along the flat, fertile valley of the river Eden was straightforward compared to building a railway across the bleak Pennine moors, and the first mineral trains ran on 8th April 1862, while passenger workings commenced two months later. Appleby folk were clearly excited by the coming of the railway (the Settle & Carlisle was some years away) and a colourful procession took place in the town, followed by a grand dinner at the King's Head hotel and a ball in the evening. Regrettably, the station (later Appleby East) was quite high up on the eastern side of town, and rather remote, which did not bode well for future passenger traffic. Latterly, the weekday service consisted of three trains between Darlington and Penrith (as previously mentioned) and this ceased in January 1962 when all passenger workings were withdrawn. After those trains ended, thrice-weekly freight workings continued from Appleby to Warcop and Hartley quarry, near Kirkby Stephen, and here Ivatt Class 4MT No.43049 creates an irresistible attraction for local children who cling enthusiastically to the crossing gates as it shunts at the former Appleby East station on 31st July 1967. Perhaps they were in the know that 1967 would be the last year for BR steam in the town! *John Goss*

Opened in 1876 by the Furness Railway, the little-known branch from Hincaster Junction to Arnside was built primarily to convey mineral traffic from the Barrow-in-Furness area to County Durham and vice versa. These trains would have traversed the West Coast Main Line from Hincaster Junction to Tebay where they would have branched off onto the line to Kirkby Stephen East and Stainmore. The line's principal engineering work was a 25-arch viaduct over the river Beela north of Sandside. A passenger service of five return trains a day was operated from the opening between Kendal and Grange-over-Sands but it ceased from 4th May 1942, presumably as a wartime economy measure. Through goods workings ended in 1963 and the Sandside to Hincaster section was lifted in 1966, the surviving stretch being retained for a further six years to serve a quarry at Sandside. On 21st May 1963 Thompson Class B1 4-6-0 No.61026 *Ourebi* powered a day excursion from Lincoln to Windermere (Lake Side) travelling via Leeds, Skipton and Carnforth to Ulverston where the train reversed. The lucky passengers were treated to a cruise on Lake Windermere while the empty stock was moved to Windermere via Arnside and Hincaster Junction. Stanier Class 5MT 4-6-0 No.44874 then hauled the train from Windermere to Arnside via Hincaster Junction where *Ourebi* was waiting to take over for the return run to Lincoln. The vast majority of participants would almost certainly have regarded the cruise as the highlight of their day, and were probably oblivious to the fact that their train was one of the last, possibly *the* last, passenger trains to traverse the Hincaster Junction to Arnside line. Here, No.44874 is seen passing the former Sandside station where a few coal wagons indicate that the goods yard was still open for business. *Noel Machell*

The Carnforth to Barrow-in-Furness line had its beginnings at the western end of the route and not, as one might expect, at Carnforth where a main line connection was made. The Dukes of Devonshire and Buccleuch had toyed with the idea of a mineral line to transport iron ore for some years but it was not until George Stephenson's ideas for a railway in the Barrow area were made known in 1837 that serious consideration was given. Plans were drawn up for a line from the iron mines at Dalton and slate quarries at Kirkby to Barrow, 15 miles in total, and the Royal Assent was received to the Furness Railway (FR) Act in May 1844 and a pier constructed for loading iron ore vessels near Barrow station. During 1848 the Kirkby branch was extended to Broughton and the Dalton branch had been continued to Ulverston. The latter town was merely a branch line terminus for three years from 1854, but became more prominent when the Ulverston & Lancaster Railway was opened in 1857. During the 1860s the FR absorbed its neighbours one by one, the Ulverston & Lancaster in 1862 while the Whitehaven & Furness Junction Railway, which opened throughout between Whitehaven and Barrow in 1850, was taken over in 1866. Meanwhile, at Barrow the FR had purchased Piel embankment and Piel pier station, on the outskirts of the town, and these were used for boat services to the Isle of Man and Belfast. Remarkably, Piel pier station was served by a through Midland Railway (MR) train which, commencing on 1st July 1867, left Leeds at 10.00am while in September of that year a further service was inaugurated from Leeds that provided a connection with a MR train from King's Cross. These services were diverted to a new dock in Barrow which was commissioned in June 1881 and the Piel branch faded from the scene, being finally laid to rest in 1936. In this portrait Stanier Class 8F No.48683 is depicted near Carnforth F&M Junction heading towards Barrow-in-Furness with a Northwich to Whitehaven train of 'Covhop' wagons on 30th April 1966. Interestingly, No.48683 was one of a batch constructed by the Southern Railway at Brighton works in 1943/44, this particular example being out-shopped in January 1944. *Noel Machell*

A delightful scene at Grange-over-Sands on 11th September 1958 as Class 5MT No.45014, working the daily Ulverston to Carnforth pick-up freight, shunts the goods yard. Note the two camping coaches parked immediately in front of the FR goods shed with the station buildings to the rear. All the buildings, with the exception of the signal box, are attractively constructed in the local Morecambe Bay limestone. The photographer points out that prior to its withdrawal in August 1957 this working was often powered by the last FR 0-6-0 in service, No.52510. *Noel Machell*

A heavy eastbound train is seen setting off from Grange-over-Sands station some time in 1962 with Class 5MT No.45351 and an unidentified BR Standard Caprotti Class 5MT in charge. The formation indicates that this may have been a through working from Workington to either Liverpool or Manchester. The 1959/60 winter timetable lists one weekday train to each destination but they were painfully slow even by the standards of the period: the 1.03pm from Workington, for example, was advertised to arrive at Manchester (Victoria) at 6.12pm after a journey of 139 miles. The train was scheduled to stop at all the minor stations along the Cumberland coast, the only exception being Eskmeals which was closed to passengers from 31st August 1959. An overnight train from Workington to London was booked to arrive at Euston at the ungodly hour of 3.51am so, perhaps, this was one occasion when passengers actually wanted their train to be late.
Alan H. Bryant / Rail Photoprints collection

This photograph, taken in August 1960, shows Fowler Class 4P 2-6-4T No.42395 running alongside the promenade with a westbound train between Grange-over-Sands and Kents Bank stations. The identity of the train is unknown but judging by the non-corridor compartment coaches it would appear to have been a purely local working. The Carnforth to Barrow-in-Furness line crosses two river estuaries on long viaducts, thus giving the railway an advantage because the nearest road crossings are much further up the rivers Kent and Leven. Note the very neat edge to the ballast: clearly the local permanent way gang took great pride in their section of line. *Rail Photoprints*

Ulverston station - an absolute gem. The station was rebuilt in 1873 for the Furness Railway (FR), the architects being Paley and Austin, and the premises are listed as being of special architectural and historical merit. Perhaps the most immediately noticeable feature of the station is the track with platforms on both sides but the buildings are the most striking and distinctive feature. The main two-storey building, built of red sandstone, has a long frontage with a tall clock tower which indicated its importance to the FR. The impressive clock tower has large ball finials on each corner of the tower parapet. The delicate glass and iron platform awnings are repeated at the front of the station. In this portrait BR Standard Class 4MT No.75048 is seen posing with a short freight train some time in the mid-1960s. It is possible that this picture was taken during the very last week of steam traction on BR as No.75048 was regularly employed on the Carnforth to Ulverston shunting turn during that week, being observed on 2nd August 1968, the last weekday of steam working. *ARPT*

During the last few years of steam traction in the north-west of England there were a number of turns for 'Britannia' Pacifics and 'Black Fives' between Barrow-in-Furness and Preston/Crewe. In late 1966 the 7.15am Barrow to Preston and 10.47am return were booked for steam traction while the 1.46pm Barrow to London (Euston) and 4.10pm Euston to Barrow were both scheduled for steam haulage north of Crewe. Here, 'Britannia' Pacific No.70002 *Geoffrey Chaucer* is seen passing through Roose station with an unidentified up passenger working in the mid-1960s. In times gone by Roose was also on the direct line from Kirkby to Piel, and a junction where the Piel line diverged from the main line but that was closed, as previously mentioned, in July 1936. The line to the original Barrow station also diverged there but the tracks were removed as long ago as 1871. *Cumbrian Railways Association*

A tight fit. The Maryport & Carlisle line is well known as one of the first railway lines in Great Britain, and this has tended to overshadow the neighbouring Whitehaven & Maryport line (later known as the Whitehaven Junction Railway) which was incorporated by an Act of Parliament on 4th July 1844. Part of this route ran along the shoreline, beneath unstable cliffs, and landslips delayed the opening throughout to Whitehaven until March 1847. This line originally terminated at Bransty station, on the northern edge of Whitehaven, but in 1852 a 1,333 yards-long tunnel was brought into use between there and Corkickle where a connection was made with the Whitehaven & Furness Junction Railway. This established a vital main line link enabling passenger and goods trains to reach Barrow and other points south thereof, the only physical connection hitherto being via the Whitehaven Harbour line. In this picture, taken during the last few months of steam activity in the area, a rather smart looking Stanier Class 8F 2-8-0, No.48151, bursts into the daylight at the southern end of the tunnel on 14th September 1967. The section of line between Barrow-in-Furness and Whitehaven was probably one of the least photographed on the BR system in steam days due to its inaccessibility and, most crucially, very early dieselisation of the passenger services. *ARPT*

Opposite bottom: The Workington area has a rich industrial heritage based on coal mines, iron foundries and steel works and all these industries suffered a long period of decline which, in the case of the iron industry, began as long ago as the 1880s as a result of competition from imported ore. Many of the dense network of local lines lost their passenger trains in the 1920s/30s and some subsequently closed completely as a result of the area's continued industrial retrenchment. In this picture Ivatt Class 4MT 2-6-0 No.43023 is depicted near Workington steel works with a goods working on 31st May 1967 and the backdrop provides a hint of the town's industrial landscape. The year 1967 was the last for steam at Workington, where the shed closed from 1st January 1968, but the shed building remained in use as a diesel unit and wagon repair depot for some years afterwards. Freight locomotives monopolised the shed's allocation in the BR steam era and in 1959 Fowler Class 4Fs and Ivatt Class 2MTs predominated, while half a dozen 'Jinty' 0-6-0Ts were also based there for shunting duties. *ARPT*

Above: The 'old' at Derwent Junction. This location, where the line from Penrith joined the Cumberland coast route, is about half a mile north of Workington (Main) station and, as its name suggests, the river Derwent was nearby but its course is hidden by an embankment. Fowler Class 4F 0-6-0 No.44461 is seen propelling a loaded coal train, that had probably originated from St. Helens colliery on the outskirts of Workington, past Derwent Junction signal box. The track of the Penrith line can be seen in the middle of this picture which dates from 7th May 1963. No.44461 was a product of Horwich works from where it emerged in May 1928 and lasted in traffic until September 1964. *Noel Machell*

The 'new' at Derwent Junction. Photographed on the same day as the previous picture, Ivatt Class 2MT 2-6-0 No.46432 pulling a coal train runs past Derwent Junction box before setting back into the docks once it was clear of the junction. The docks, which were accessed using the tracks on the right of the shot, were privately owned and white gates indicate the boundary between BR and the dock estate. No.46432, a much more modern design than No.44461 seen in the previous shot, was built at Crewe and dated from December 1948. It was in service for less than 20 years, being withdrawn from traffic in mid-1967. Examples of this class were constructed well into the 1950s and some of those were only in service for as little as eleven years. *Noel Machell*

The lines radiating from the border city of Carlisle are among some of the most attractive and photogenic in Great Britain, the only exception being the route to Workington which runs along the flat, and relatively uninteresting, Solway coastal plain. The 28 miles-long section from Carlisle to Maryport was opened by the Maryport & Carlisle Railway on a piecemeal basis between July 1840 and February 1845, while the stretch between Maryport and Workington dates from January 1846. In this photograph Class 4F 0-6-0 No.44125 is seen emitting a volcanic smoke effect as it crosses the river Caldew at Cummersdale with an evening Carlisle yard to Workington freight in August 1964.
Peter Robinson

The Whitehaven Cleator & Egremont Railway, one of the dense network of local lines in West Cumberland, received the Royal Assent on 16th June 1854 for a line from Mirehouse Junction, south of Whitehaven, to Egremont with a branch to Cleator Moor and Frizington. The initial sections of the line opened on 1st July 1857 and the Egremont route was extended southwards to make a connection with the Furness Railway at Sellafield, that stretch of route opening on 2nd August 1869. The line to Frizington was also extended and opened in stages to Lamplugh and Marron Junction, a new station on the Workington to Penrith route, the final section opening on 2nd April 1866. In this shot, taken at Cleator Moor on 7th May 1963, the local coal merchant is very busy in the goods yard loading his *ex*-army Bedford truck with bagged coal for local delivery while Ivatt Class 4MT No.43004 passes through with the 12.10pm Rowrah to Moor Row train. This is formed of mineral wagons loaded with a very pure grade of limestone destined for use in the United Steel Company's furnaces at Moss Bay works, Workington. *Noel Machell*

Moor Row was the operational hub of the routes immediately south-east of Whitehaven, tracks fanning out in four directions to Workington (Siddick Junction), Whitehaven, Rowrah and Sellafield. In this illustration the train seen in the previous shot is depicted at Moor Row station where the line to Sellafield can be seen diverging sharply from the route to Cleator Moor by the signal box. In more prosperous days there used to be a locomotive depot here, located on the extreme left of the picture, but it was closed in the mid-1950s. Moor Row station had a chequered history, the lines to Workington (Siddick Junction) and Camerton (Marron West Junction), on the Workington to Penrith line, both closing to passengers on 13th April 1931, while the route to Sellafield was closed to passenger traffic on 7th January 1935. Services were reinstated on the last-mentioned route, however, from 6th May 1946 for schoolchildren attending classes in Egremont and, latterly, a workmen's service was run for employees of the Sellafield (Calder Hall) Nuclear Plant. Regular services were reportedly withdrawn in September 1965 but sporadic passenger workings apparently continued until 3rd March 1969. A set of coaches was retained for these services and this is visible in one of the sidings on the left of the picture. *Noel Machell*

The spectacular Workington to Penrith route through the Lake District was the result of enterprising schemes by two separate companies over a 20-year period. The first section to be constructed was that between the port of Workington and the market town of Cockermouth, which was promoted by the Cockermouth & Workington Railway and sanctioned on 21st July 1845. The line, which followed the course of the river Derwent, opened on 28th April 1847 and initially had four intermediate stations. It was considered that an eastwards extension towards the Durham coalfield would be of immense benefit to the Cumberland iron industry because it would enable high-quality Durham coking coal to reach local furnaces, while in the reverse direction iron ore would flow eastwards to the north-east of England. Various abortive schemes were put forward, but in 1860 a group of local landowners and industrialists combined to promote the Cockermouth Keswick and Penrith Railway (CK&PR), and their prospectus enthusiastically set out the route's undoubted potential for carrying heavy mineral and passenger traffic. An Act for the construction of the line was obtained on 1st August 1861 and at a meeting during the following year shareholders were advised that construction would soon commence. The line opened on 1st November 1864 for mineral traffic and 2nd January 1865 for passengers. The operation of mineral trains at the Penrith end was made much smoother by a spur between the CK&PR and cross-Pennine Stainmore line which obviated the need to reverse at Penrith. The boom years did not last for long, however, as imported minerals and new steel making processes led to a decline in the Cumberland iron industry and consequently a loss of traffic on the Lake District line. Furthermore, in the 1920s competition from local buses started to erode the route's passenger traffic and after the Second World War this was compounded by the advent of private motoring. Closure of the section west of Keswick occurred in 1966 while the remaining part of the route struggled on until it, too, was shut in 1972. Here, Ivatt 2-6-0 Class 2MT No.46432 is seen at Cockermouth station on a snowy 2nd April 1966. *ARPT*

The final steam passenger workings over the remaining stub of the Workington to Penrith line are thought to have occurred in July 1967, just five months before steam working was eliminated completely from the Carlisle area. On 15th July a brace of filthy Ivatt Class 4MT 2-6-0s, Nos.43120 and 43121, were rostered to work the Keswick Convention special, which had originated in London, from Penrith to Keswick. The pair are depicted at Keswick, presumably running round before taking the empty stock to Carlisle. The return train a week later was also expected to be steam worked and enthusiasts expended considerable 'elbow grease' on sprucing up No.43139's blistered paintwork in the expectation that it would work the train. They must have been bitterly disappointed, however, when a diesel locomotive was also booked for the duty and, to add insult to injury, the diesel piloted No.43139, thus ruining any prospect of a decent photograph. Please also refer to a previous picture taken at Penrith.
Chris Davies / Rail Photoprints collection

Life for the signalman at the tiny Bassenthwaite Lake station could not have been unduly stressful and here he is seen waiting to hand the token to the crew of Ivatt Class 2MT 2-6-0 No.46488 hauling a pick-up goods train on 14th August 1959. Situated virtually on the shore of the lake in an idyllic setting, the beautifully kept station was as pretty as one would wish to see with neatly tended flower beds and hedgerows. The staff there had a reasonable amount of time to pursue horticultural activity between trains which, in the 1959 summer timetable, numbered about nine in each direction on weekdays with just four on Sundays. The main train of the day was 'The Lakes Express' which ran to and from London Euston during the height of the summer and stopped at Bassenthwaite Lake station. It is likely that much of the passenger traffic was seasonal and the line was probably quiet during the winter months while, on the freight side, the derisory length of No.46488's train gives a clue to the route's declining fortunes. Sadly, the fabulous scenery and relaxed lifestyle for staff did little to impress Doctor Beeching's accountants and, after being cut back to Keswick, the line was closed completely in 1972 as previously mentioned. *ARPT*

The unrivalled Lake District. The railway crosses and recrosses the river Greta many times between Threlkeld and Keswick and here the majestic Saddleback mountain (also known as Blencathra) forms the backdrop as a couple of unidentified Ivatt Class 2MT 2-6-0s head for Keswick with the 11.10am from Carlisle on Whit Monday 1963. *ARPT*

The London-bound 'The Lakes Express' crosses Mosedale viaduct behind Stanier Class 4MT 2-6-4T No.42594 on 19th August 1961. This was the crack train of the day on the Workington to Penrith line, and in the summer 1959 timetable it left Workington at 8.55am on Mondays to Fridays, being scheduled to arrive at Euston at 5.40pm. On Saturdays its departure time from the Cumberland town was 8.40am and advertised arrival time in London was 5.10pm. The slightly faster schedule on Saturdays was due to the fact that the train omitted some stops south of Preston and was only allowed eight minutes at Crewe, presumably to change engines, whereas on weekdays passengers had plenty of time to admire Crewe station's delights, nineteen minutes being booked for the change of motive power. A portion from Windermere, attached at Oxenholme, was also conveyed and that included a restaurant car so travellers would have been able to obtain a meal during the long journey. *Bob Leslie/Peter Robinson collection*

Ivatt Class 2MT 2-6-0 No.46426 makes a spirited exit from Penrith with the Workington portion of 'The Lakes Express' in June 1965. There had been fears that the train would not run during the 1965 summer season and to celebrate its reprieve Carlisle Upperby shed turned out a specially cleaned locomotive on the first day of its operation. There was a steep climb from Penrith to Penruddock and the crew would have no doubt preferred to take a 'run' at the bank, but the need to slow to pick up the tablet at Penrith No.1 signal box made life difficult and they would have to hope their engine was not short of breath on the climb. *Peter Robinson*

The station nameboard immediately identifies the location of this photograph which was taken on 28th July 1964. Stanier Class 4MT 2-6-4T No.42449 waits in the loop platform at Oxenholme which was bi-directional and normally used by Windermere branch trains; the tracks of the West Coast Main Line are on the right. The 10 miles-long branch from Oxenholme to Windermere was authorised in 1845 and the first section, as far as Kendal, came into use on 22nd September 1846 and the rest of the line was opened on 20th April 1847. In the 1964/65 winter timetable a service of nine trains was advertised on weekdays along the branch, including one train in each direction to/from London Euston. On Sundays the timetable advertised only one service each way in the evening, this apparently being a Ribble bus operating a scheduled local service for which, according to the small print in the timetable, rail passengers had to obtain supplementary tickets prior to the day of travel. Presumably rail passengers who turned up without the necessary ticket were asked to pay the bus fare in addition to their train fare. *Ian Turnbull/Rail Photoprints*

The 3.15pm Windermere to Lancaster train, with Fairburn Class 4MT 2-6-4T No.42299 in charge, gets under way from its Kendal stop and resumes the climb to Oxenholme on 25th September 1964. This locomotive was one of many that had a relatively short working life: it was out-shopped from Derby works in December 1947 and taken out of service in March 1965, six months after this shot was taken. Note the coaches forming the train which are a real assortment of BR Standard, LMS and LNER design. *Noel Machell*

The distant Lakeland fells provide a stunning backdrop to this illustration of Stanier 'Jubilee' Class 6P5F No.45592 *Indore* coasting along with a short goods working just south of Staveley in the mid-1960s. The vehicle formed immediately behind the locomotive is a BR Standard Full Brake coach, known in railwaymen's parlance as a BG. The train has just passed the level crossing where the line crosses the main road between Windermere and Kendal and one can imagine long queues of traffic particularly on busy Bank Holidays when people flocked to the lakes. The fell nearest to the camera rises to a maximum height of just over 700 feet above sea level, modest by Lake District standards, but those in the far distance are nearly twice that height. *Cumbrian Railways Association*

Photographed on a typically misty Lakeland day, an unidentified Stanier Class 4MT 2-6-4T makes a brisk departure from Windermere station in the mid-1960s with a local train formed mainly of non-corridor compartment stock. Discerning passengers would probably have opted to travel in the fourth vehicle in the formation with the white, oval toilet windows, this being a more comfortable LNER Thompson-designed main line carriage. Judging by the 16-ton mineral wagons scattered around the goods yard the local coal merchant was kept busy and obviously maintained healthy stocks of fuel in case the supply was interrupted. Following the cessation of steam operations at Carlisle in December 1967, for a brief period prior to the end of BR steam Windermere was the most northerly point reached by steam traction. Locomotives from Carnforth shed worked the daily pick-up goods train and the photographic possibilities on the branch attracted many enthusiasts. *Cumbrian Railways Association*

Copper had been mined in the hills above Coniston for many years and until the coming of the railway it was transported by horse-drawn cart to Coniston Water, where it was transferred onto a barge, and then laboriously carted again to Broughton-in-Furness. The main Furness Railway (FR) line from Barrow-in-Furness to Broughton was opened in February 1848 and section northwards to Whitehaven in October 1850. The first proposal for a branch line to Coniston was made in 1849 for a narrow gauge line but nothing came of this and eight years elapsed before the Coniston Railway Act was passed on 10th August 1857. The builders were a local firm, Child & Pickles, but they went bankrupt, the FR taking over and opening the line on 18th June 1859. In 1860 the line was extended about a mile beyond Coniston to serve the copper and slate mines. The FR recognised the line's tourist potential and purchased a steam yacht *Gondola* in 1859 and later bought another vessel, *Lady of the Lake*. In the 1930s a service of ten daily trains was timetabled and in 1939 a direct train

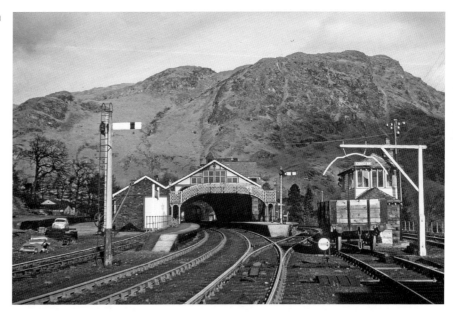

from and to Blackpool was added to the service but this probably only served to emphasise that most of the line's traffic was of a seasonal nature. The harsh economic situation that was facing BR in the 1950s resulted in a closure proposal and subsequently this idyllic backwater was closed to passengers from 6th October 1958, and goods from 30th April 1962. A Lancaster architect, E.G. Paley, designed a delightful terminal station at Coniston in Swiss chalet style which was located close to the lake and is seen here in the early 1960s. *Gavin Morrison*

The Coniston branch diverged from the Barrow-in-Furness to Whitehaven main line at Foxfield station which is situated by the sands at the head of the river Duddon estuary. Foxfield is a peaceful, pretty little station with a small stone-built train shed (since demolished) over the down platform and stationmaster's house on the up side which is partially visible behind the train in this photograph. Note the vintage platform seat with (what appears to be) a moulding of a rabbit in the iron framework, oil lamps and old LMS style station nameboard. The train is a standard LMS two-coach pull-push formation with Ivatt Class 2MT No.41217 the motive power. *Cumbrian Railways Association*

Few routes featured in this book have had such fluctuating fortunes as the Lake Side (Windermere) to Ulverston line. The line from Ulverston along the estuary of the river Leven to Newby Bridge was first proposed by the Furness Railway (FR) and the first sod was ceremonially cut by the company's General Manager, James Ramsden, at Haverthwaite on 22nd November 1866. The FR soon realised the tourist potential and commercial benefit of a connection to Lake Side and an extension was duly opened on 1st June 1869, just in time for the summer season. The company constructed a quay at Lake Side to enable quick and easy transfer between trains and the steamers. The advent of railways had widened the horizons of the more prosperous Victorians who used the train to reach Lake Windermere and then took a relaxing trip on the lake as part of a day out. There was also substantial goods traffic on the branch, including iron ore for Backbarrow iron works, near Haverthwaite, and coal for the lake steamers. In 1872 the FR purchased the company running the steamers and during the period up to the start of the First World War the Ulverston to Lake Side branch enjoyed a wonderful period of prosperity conveying train loads of happy day trippers in the summer months. The development of road transport, however, started to knock the gloss off the line's balance sheet and a gradual decline culminated in the inevitable decision in 1938 to cease passenger operations during the winter months. The passenger service was withdrawn entirely for the duration of the Second World War. After hostilities had ended, services resumed but much of the line's holiday traffic had been lost to coach travel, which was increasingly popular, and the growth in private motoring. BR enterprisingly laid on a summer seasonal service from Morecambe to Lake Side, for which a Fairburn 2-6-4T from Lancaster (Green Ayre) shed was normally rostered, and distinctive destination boards were made and displayed on every coach: No.42136 is depicted just west of Newby Bridge powering one of those trains on 17th June 1962. Alas, it was all to no avail and BR sought to close the line to passenger traffic and this occurred from 6th September 1965, though freight continued until April 1967. The small station at Newby Bridge had a charmed life, being 'temporarily' closed from 12th September 1939, the closure being made permanent from 12th July 1949. Following closure, the southern section of the line was requisitioned for a road improvement scheme but the remaining part was taken over by a preservation society which brought Newby Bridge station back to life after more than 30 years of disuse. *Noel Machell*